# RAISING BILINGUAL BAMBINI

**Also by Eric Dregni**
**Published by the University of Minnesota Press**

*By the Waters of Minnetonka*

*For the Love of Cod: A Father and Son's Search for Norwegian Happiness*

*In Cod We Trust: Living the Norwegian Dream*

*Let's Go Fishing! Fish Tales from the North Woods*

*Midwest Marvels: Roadside Attractions Across Iowa, Minnesota, the Dakotas, and Wisconsin*

*Minnesota Marvels: Roadside Attractions in the Land of Lakes*

*Never Trust a Thin Cook and Other Lessons from Italy's Culinary Capital*

*Vikings in the Attic: In Search of Nordic America*

*You're Sending Me Where? Dispatches from Summer Camp*

# Raising Bilingual Bambini

## THE ART OF IMMERSING OUR FAMILY IN LA DOLCE VITA

ERIC DREGNI

MIN NE SO TA
University of Minnesota Press
Minneapolis
London

All photographs are courtesy of the author.



Published by the University of Minnesota Press
111 Third Avenue South, Suite 290
Minneapolis, MN 55401-2520
http://www.upress.umn.edu

ISBN 978-1-5179-2132-3 (hc)
ISBN 978-1-5179-2303-7 (pb)

A Cataloging-in-Publication record for this book is available from the Library of Congress.

Printed in the United States of America on acid-free paper



35 34 33 32 31 30 29 28 27 26 10 9 8 7 6 5 4 3 2 1

*To our kids, Eilif, Otto, and Astri, for going along on this lifelong adventure. I'm sorry if my "experiment" to make you fluent in Italian put you in a spotlight that you didn't ask for. Mostly, though, thanks to Katy for putting up with my obsession with traveling and using my family as the subject. Perhaps I'm a bit starry-eyed, but I wanted us to read and remember the fun we had.*

# CONTENTS

## III. BRINGING IT ALL BACK HOME

# PREFACE

## Let's Get Married!

"Let's go to Rome to get engaged," Katy announces. It's a lazy Sunday afternoon as we sit around our apartment in the center of Modena, Italy, reading the *International Herald Tribune*. We've been dating for three years, two of those spent in this culinary capital feasting on tortellini, paper-thin prosciutto, and balsamic vinegar on just about anything we can find in the fridge or pantry. We struggle to pay for our grocery bills from my freelancing for local Italian newspapers and our teaching English to anyone who can stand our Minnesotan accents.

We've come to a crossroads. How do the two of us go forward? Do we stay in Italy and always remain foreigners, the immigrants, the *extracomunitari*, the non-European Union invaders? Or do we move back home for more opportunities and give up the international experience of living abroad in Italy?

We can scarcely afford our gorgeous apartment in Modena built in the fourteenth century originally as a nunnery. No Italian would touch this apartment, as it brings with it a double dose of bad luck: No one can curse you like dead nuns, and some would say we're desecrating a sacred spot by living in sin together before marriage. We're not so worried. Still, we have little chance to advance here without proper work permits.

Instead, we flee our dilemma and blow our savings on five days in a luxurious Roman bed-and-breakfast with the Holy See looking down on us. The second day, a terrible flu strikes Katy, and she is bedridden in the plush featherbed. I wander the streets of Rome in search of lunch to bring back to her. What fun is it weaving through these charming alleys alone? The thought strikes me: What would I do without Katy? We've had three fantastic years together, and I never want them to end.

I race up the two flights of steps to our B & B armed with delicious *panini* of mozzarella, speck, and arugula. Katy rises from her slumber, her nose red from blowing it and eyes puffy from sickness. I tell her about my epiphany, that I want to spend the rest of my life with her. Would she marry me?

"What? You're asking me now, when I'm sick? No, no, no, no, no!" This serves as a shot in the arm; she jumps out of bed. "No, no. This won't do at all." She puts on her clothes, ignores the sandwiches, and is ready to go. "I don't want to get engaged while phlegm is dripping out of me and I can barely breathe!"

As if Katy is injected with adrenaline, we crisscross the center of Rome. I propose in front of the Trevi Fountain as we toss coins over our shoulders into the gurgling water. I propose at Santa Maria del Trastevere in front of a chorus of kids from Iowa in red bandannas (whom the Italians assume are communists). I ask again at the Colosseum, which isn't particularly romantic considering the slaughters that have taken place there. I propose at the Pantheon under the beam of light shining through the oculus in the ceiling. Finally, I propose on the Ponte Sant'Angelo, the bridge over the Tiber River by the pope's Castel Sant'Angelo with all of Bernini's ecstatic angel statues gazing down on us.

"Yeah . . . I guess I'll marry you," Katy shrugs, leaving me to wonder if she has second thoughts.

When we return to Modena, we tell our Italian friends that we are now engaged. They laugh. Fiorella at the market below our apartment quips, "As if you weren't engaged before! You joker." I realize the word *fidanzata* signifies both girlfriend and fiancée in Italian. As Katy and I are living together, of course we're already engaged by Italian standards.

Events always go backward with us. Rather than enjoy our honeymoon on a grand tour of Italy, we've already visited Venice and had a room with a view in Florence. Katy announces, let's go home to America to get married.

Back from Italy, I can't stop making Italian hand gestures when I speak. My friends at home can't tell if these are rude. They're further confused when I try to break the habit by hiding my hands behind my back.

The typical conversation goes something like this.

"How was your time in Italy?"

"Great . . . Yeah, it was really great . . ." Followed by an uncomfortable pause. I have so many stories to tell but can't sum up our experiences in chitchat. I've almost forgotten how to converse in English.

"OK . . . enough said," they say. "What are you doing tonight?"

Katy and I are married officially a year after our return—with no funds left for a honeymoon. I dream of returning to Italy someday. Instead, I win a Fulbright fellowship to Norway at the same time we discover Katy is pregnant. Our new addition is born in the remote fjord town of Orkanger, just a couple hundred miles south of the Arctic Circle.

I look at our beautiful boy and wonder about all the trials and tribulations that await him. I want our son to be a citizen of the world, but how can we share our international experiences with him? I resolve that we will bring him, and any other kids that follow, to live in Italy. Katy goes along with my plan, realizing that she doesn't have to commit since it's financially impossible at the moment.

To see some sunlight, we find a cheap charter flight from Norway to Italy. I assumed that Eilif would be a dual citizen, but the Norwegian government doesn't automatically give citizenship to babies born on its soil. In fact, he has no citizenship, so we quickly apply for a passport with the US embassy in Oslo. At two weeks of age, Eilif has no country and can't even keep his head up for a passport photo. I have to hold him over my shoulder with my hand behind his head.

We visit friends in Modena, and they dote over our newborn because oversized Italian families are now rare. The Modenese women look longingly at our baby, and we can't help but be proud. Well-dressed Italian mothers look over Katy up and down and say "*Complimenti!*" to signal their approval with her postpregnancy appearance.

When our vacation is over, we return to the frozen north. Our indulgence in fresh tortellini, prosciutto, and Lambrusco is over. I then vow that we will return to Italy someday to share our experiences with Eilif.

I want to save our son all the struggles we endured in learning Italian—all the flash cards and tedious memorization of verb charts. I've failed at becoming fluent in Norwegian, despite a year of classes. I imagine our baby Eilif being able to switch languages easily without suffering through hours of studying.

He doesn't speak anything yet, so perhaps we can brainwash him to be bilingual, or even trilingual. We resolve to expose Eilif to the world, even once we're back in the middle of America. Can we provide him with a global perspective and the gift of a second language? Can we instill a wanderlust in him so he'll want to travel with us?

After a year in Norway, we are returning home yet again to the United States. This time it's different. Not only have we adopted a more stoic Scandinavian demeanor, but we have a baby. We recognize we may not be able to travel again soon, but our real adventure is just beginning.

# PART I

# Birthing Bilingual Bambini

## LIE TO YOUR CHILDREN

My parents made a vow to each other that they would live abroad. With three kids in tow, they managed to bring us overseas for a year in England and two in Belgium. They gave us a passport to the world. Now I want to do the same thing and pass on this worldview to Eilif.

In the meantime, we move back from Norway to the center of North America—to Minnesota, as far into English-speaking territory as one can get in this world. Even so, we're in Minneapolis, where dozens of other languages whiz by us, but rarely Italian. Each neighborhood has different ethnicities, different cultures.

Downtown, I meet an Italian teacher from Ticino, the Italian-speaking canton of Switzerland. She met her Greek husband in Geneva, where French is spoken. He speaks to their daughter in Greek, the mother in Italian, and French is the common language between the parents because they had lived in a French-speaking canton of Switzerland. The little girl understands all three languages; she also knows English from her American school, where she has Spanish lessons too. Now the family is moving back to northern Switzerland, where

German is spoken. Amazingly, the five-year-old girl can switch languages without a glitch. If they can manage this linguistic feat, we should be able to at least introduce one second language to our prodigal son.

I read up on language experiments. The Holy Roman Emperor Frederick II of Sicily yearned to discover which was the true divine language that kids would speak if their parents didn't push them in one direction. Would it be Latin, Greek, or Hebrew? He kept two infants separated from people to observe which language would come naturally, a sort of medieval Skinner box. The children died.

We don't follow Frederick's lead and instead opt to expose them to as many cultures as possible. Eilif's preschool teacher Vicki tells us, "Kids can learn as many languages as people can speak to them." Apparently the trick is to start them young.

I want to teach Eilif the language of his great-great-grandfather, Norwegian, but my language skills are terrible, partly because all the Norwegians we met in our year in Trondheim spoke perfect English. My grandparents didn't pass on their Swedish and Norwegian to their offspring in the United States due to the xenophobic madness of World War I. Signs from the US government in Scandinavian halls in Minnesota warned: DON'T BE SUSPECTED! USE AMERICAN LANGUAGE. AMERICA IS OUR HOME. Holding on to those antiquated Old World languages only brought accusations of espionage down on the Germans. Besides, Katy says I look ludicrous when I fumble through Norwegian.

Instead, we agree that I will speak only Italian, and she will talk to Eilif in English. This way, he'll understand his American teachers when he starts school. Studies show that you can never start speaking a foreign language too early to kids; some even say that fetuses process words in the womb. But even a language geek like me didn't dare chat with Katy's giant pregnant belly in Italian.

Some studies find that bilingual kids speak later than others. Fortunately, Eilif can't stop talking. He learns that with his mother, it's English, and with me, Italian. One day he asks why I speak differently than everyone else. I explain that I lost my English when we lived in Modena and can only speak Italian now. (A white lie: By the time he uncovers the truth, he'll be able to speak Italian.) Therefore, he needs to help his idiot of a father relearn English.

People out in public tend to have a less sympathetic reaction. At the Target store on Lake Street in Minneapolis, a middle-aged woman with oversized sunglasses smiles at Eilif and me as we are buying a Crock-Pot. (Note to self: Never again buy Katy cookware for her birthday.) I imagine the woman ahead of us in line must think it's cute to see a father shopping with his son, especially if I'm teaching him to be a little chef. When Eilif and I speak Italian to each other, though, the woman's expression sours and twists. She eyes me and complains to the cashier about immigrants taking all the jobs in the United States. They can't even speak "American." The cashier smiles forgivingly. Moments later I break into English to speak to the cashier. The woman blushes and scurries out of the store.

My parents, on the other hand, think I'm just plain crazy. "He's going to be so confused," my father warns. "He won't understand a thing!" I remind my dad that they put me in a French-language school in Brussels for kindergarten and first grade. This gave me a love of languages as if they were a secret code, a connection, between people. They could communicate in ways that others couldn't understand.

At first, my mother wants to give away the secret to Eilif that I do indeed speak English. But she finally goes along with the ruse, explaining to Eilif, "Your papà needs some English lessons from his grandmother too. We'll help him out."

The irony is that Eilif hears me speaking English all the time to Katy and everyone else. Directly to him, though, I only speak Italian. Somehow, he accepts this disconnect.

Other relatives view our endeavor as a curiosity. Katy's brother Rob thinks it's fantastic to have a secret language that no one else can understand.

Katy's step-grandfather asks, "So now that you've lived in It-ly for a few years, I suppose you speak italics, right?"

His embarrassed wife corrects him, "It's not italics! It's eye-talian!"

Our families struggle to accept our odd experiment, but at least they don't openly mock it. One day, two-year-old Eilif picks up a piece of a baguette and gives part of it to Katy. "Bread!" he proclaims. Then he turns to me: "*Pane!*" Back and forth he repeats, "*Pane.* Bread. *Pane.* Bread." He gets it.

## NO MORE BARGAIN BABIES

As soon as Eilif starts talking, he takes a cue from Julius Caesar and refers to himself in the third person for all his demands. He calls himself "Eilif the Boy." Katy is "Eilif's mom." Strangely enough, I now refer to myself as "Eilif's dad" when talking with other parents. At first, I worry that I'm losing my identity but believe that I'm gaining so much more. I see myself reflected back in him.

Still, his booming vocal range is challenged only by his newfound pleasure of pounding objects to see how much sound he can produce. He tells Katy, "Mamma, Eilif doesn't want pretty toys for Christmas. Eilif wants loud ones. Ones that go BANG! BANG!"

Eilif takes a break from his hubbub to go over to his mamma, point to her belly, and exclaim, "Baby!"

Katy is amazed: "How does he know?" Indeed, Katy has just taken a pregnancy test and is expecting.

I joke with friends, "Katy got herself pregnant again . . . I didn't do it!" She is not amused.

While I'm thrilled and terrified to have a second child, I know that my plans to return to Italy are now doubly as difficult. We'll have to wait several years to eat gelato in the piazza again.

The ultrasound for our impending baby reveals a bright spot on his heart. The doctor notes casually, "Hmm . . . it's probably nothing, but you never know." We panic as the doctor tells us we could do an amniocentesis, a process that would inject a needle into the uterus to test the amniotic fluid to determine if the baby will have Down's syndrome. Terrifying. The needle could put the fetus at risk and might even produce a false positive.

We have sleepless nights as we're left with this dilemma. Ultimately, Katy decides to skip the test. We don't know what we would do with the information anyway.

After the visit to the doctor, we picnic at our friend Carol's house. She's hosting an Indian swami, who seems oddly detached from the party. He would rather go watch the planes land at the airport, his favorite pastime. Katy asks him if he has any advice or insight into our baby.

"Pull my finger," he says. Katy understands he's not playing a fart joke on her, but this is the swami's way of connecting and understanding the situation.

Katy pulls his finger. He pronounces, "Your baby will be fine." We breathe a sigh of relief, but I question the validity of finger-pulling to predict fetus viability.

On top of this stress, Eilif keeps making noise by pushing his wagon back and forth in our apartment. Our grouchy ninety-three-year-old Norwegian landlady telephones us. "You gotta move out! The neighbors downstairs can't stand all the fuss you're making," she screeches. "Get out and buy a house!"

I'm sure this isn't legal, but Katy says it is pointless to fight her since we'd have to raise our son in this toxic environment.

This elderly landlady would make our lives miserable, plus she might be right. We need a house for our growing family.

In south Minneapolis, we discover a bungalow in need of work, one in which musicians lived amid rooms painted black, Jimi Hendrix posters, and "ZZ Top" scrawled on the walls. For the first time in our lives, we have a space to call our own—as long as we keep up with our mortgage payments.

We redo our porch and replace the impenetrable doors with glass doors to let in the light so we're not living in a prison. We discover, wedged into the old mailbox, an abandoned letter from the 1930s written in Swedish. I tell Katy that this is a sign we should speak a Scandinavian language to our kids. She's not convinced but at least puts up with my speaking Italian to Eilif.

In our bathroom, Katy relaxes in the tub to ease the pain of pregnancy—perhaps she is practicing for a water birth. I'm not sure that immersing a newborn in water is such a good plan, but she assures me that "babies aren't breathing anyway when they come out."

Although I'm excited to have a second child to converse with in Italian, our economic worries will double. I calculate the impending financial hit. Studies show that parents pay more than $400,000 to raise one child, not including college. When Eilif was born in Norway, the Norwegian government paid all the medical expenses including a $150 taxi ride each way. They put both of us up in the hospital for five nights. If Katy had been working in Norway before the birth, she would have gotten a year off work with 80 percent of her salary paid by the government. Instead, the Norwegian government paid us $5,000 to help with the baby and an extra $150 a month as child support until Eilif reached eighteen years of age. When we returned to the United States, the Norwegian government kept depositing money into our account. I wrote to the health administration in Oslo explaining that we had left the country and to stop sending us all their money. I multiplied $150 by twelve months by eighteen years and recognized I should have kept my mouth shut.

Here in the United States we have the opposite: The deductible on our insurance is $5,800, almost an $11,000 difference from having a baby in Norway. We have no luxurious taxi ride to the hospital. Instead, when Katy's water breaks, we drop Eilif off for a sleepover at my brother's, who promises to spoil him with flapjacks. I nervously load up our little blue Honda Civic with an overnight bag. I grind the gears (I've forgotten how to drive) as Katy laughs at my nervousness.

"Don't you remember what the Norwegian midwives warned?" I ask a little too excitedly. "They told us we should be very, very close to a hospital next time since the baby will come fast?"

"Just relax," Katy assures me.

I manage to park downtown, without incident, outside the old Swedish hospital. We stand aside as paramedics help a man dripping blood from a head wound onto a gurney.

We search for the midwifery unit but lose our way through the concrete corridors. I breathe slowly to avoid hyperventilating and refrain from running through the maze. A group of sickly patients wander the narrow halls pushing metal contraptions holding up their IVs, and we barely squeeze Katy's giant belly by them.

After aimless wandering, I'm comforted to hear the familiar, agonizing screams of delivering mothers. The door to the midwife wing is locked, however. A sign asks us to "Ring at the OB/GYN Unit down the hall." We walk to that door and ring the bell for a doctor. Once again, we wait. I wonder if we'll ever get in. Piped-in Muzak over the intercom does not relax us. Now even Katy is tense. "I wanted midwives, not a doctor!"

Several minutes later, the receptionist opens the doors and reports, "Babies are born in bunches. Today is a busy day." She calmly brings us to a room and tells us to make ourselves comfortable.

I hold my thoughts until after she leaves. "Get comfortable?" I ask Katy. "I'm not exactly interested in lounging around."

"It'll be fine," Katy hopes, but I can see she's no longer convinced.

A midwife knocks lightly on the door and pokes her head in. "Hi there, how is everyone? What can we do for you today?"

Katy looks at her, confused. "Um, I'm here to have a baby. Soon!"

"Great. Well, let's see what point we're at," the midwife calmly whispers. Katy puts on a starched hospital gown and tries to figure out if it should open from the front or the back.

The midwife slowly examines her and confirms my fears. "Oh my, you are just about ready!" I feel vindicated as another midwife quickly brings in the birthing tub. "I'm not sure if we'll even have time to blow this up and fill it with water. This baby may not wait!"

Disappointed that the water birth may not be feasible, Katy somehow slows down her labor long enough for us to prepare the pool. She has no time for epidural anesthesia, but the warm water relaxes her. Within an hour, after a lot of pushing, a little head pops out and a baby boy swims into the world. At least, this is how it looks to me; Katy has other thoughts on the process.

The midwives cut the cord, and an exhausted Katy cuddles her little one. The nurses clean up the newborn. All my worries about how we will provide for our infant—and if we will now be permanently stuck at home—melt away as I look into our baby's beautiful brown eyes. He looks up at us as if he knows us already and he's ready to be our son.

The nurses break my trance by asking Katy if she'd like a breather without the baby so she can rest up. I'm confused, since we've only just met him.

"We can do that?" Katy wonders out loud. This will be our first few hours in nearly two years without a child to wake us up. We fall asleep, but our dreams are shattered by the nurses who knock on the door to check Katy's vitals, see if she is hungry, or ask, "How are you doing?" We'd be doing better if we could just sleep.

In the hospital in Norway, the midwives let the new mothers come to them to check blood pressure or visit the food cart in the dining area. The Norwegians even gave us a large double bed, rather than leaving me curled up on a squeaky fake leather chair for the night. They placed the baby right between us to sleep—a no-no in the United States. Some recovering mothers would stay for a week in the Norwegian hospital that would provide full meals and help take care of the infants. On top of that, the Norwegian government pays nurses to make house calls to families with new babies and make sure everything is running smoothly.

Perhaps US hospitals intentionally make the bland food a bit mushy and the beds a bit bumpy to push the patients out. Besides, our insurance covers only twenty-four hours in the hospital.

Before we pack up the next morning, my parents call and ask, "What's your new baby's name?"

"Otto."

"No, really," my dad laughs. "What did you name him?"

"Otto," I repeat. "It's a palindrome."

"You're always teasing us, aren't you? You joker!" Neither of my parents believe me; they associate the name with Otto von Bismarck or the Kaiser as if we're breeding an Aryan super race. I point out that his name means "eight" in Italian, a numeral that when put on its side is the symbol for infinity.

That morning, my brother brings two-year-old Eilif to the hospital to visit little Otto. We have a brand-new yellow soccer ball that we tell him his baby brother has brought for him. Eilif doesn't question that a newborn was unlikely to purchase a large ball and bring it to him from inside his mother; he's not even particularly curious about the ball at all. Instead, he points at baby Otto, holds out his hands, and demands, "Have it!" He wants us to turn over his little brother to him because he is ready to put him to work.

## THE GLUT OF STUFF

At three years old, Eilif is unimpressed by everything. He's bored by the pop-up book of Vesuvius exploding and killing everyone in Pompeii.

I show him books about gladiators and mini versions of the Colosseum.

Uninterested.

Eilif only wants to watch videos, so we purchase the Italian BBC language series of *Muzzy* for kids. As the boys move past the toddler stage, I read them Italian books and play them Italian music, but I'm never quite sure how much they are absorbing. I show Eilif a shape sorter and tell him the Italian names of squares, circles, and stars that he's supposed to put inside. Eilif clumsily tries to squeeze the square blocks into the round hole. Rather than fiddle with it, he just pulls the top off and dumps all the shapes inside. He rigs the system. We did want the stupid shapes inside, right?

Eilif is not a rule follower, so we relish the quiet when he finally goes to bed. Tonight, though, it's a bit too quiet. I peek into his room on the second story, but he's not in his bed. Instead, he is sound asleep in the window well above his bed with only the screen holding him inside. The mosquito mesh of the screen could easily break, so I carefully put him back in his bed before he rolls down the roof. I don't think the gutter would catch him. He snuggles with his stuffed polar bear like a little angel.

I tell Katy, but she's barely fazed because it's always an emergency at our house. There's no instruction manual for new parents. Even if there were one, new parents have no time to read.

Katy and I try to convince ourselves our lives will stay the same as before the madness of kids. We used to be able to pack up our belongings easily and live in Italy or Norway, but this glut of stuff that comes with kids fills our house. Our lives are so enriched with the boys, but it's so much responsibility.

I still dream of living abroad, but this is getting further out of reach with every new gift that enters our house. My creative writing teacher, Julie at the University of Minnesota, tells me that it's best to go when the kids are still "portable." I make plans to pack up, but an avalanche of toys descends on our formerly quiet house.

When guests without children visit, they assume our lives are still calm and carefree. As Otto turns two years old and Eilif four, we have some kid-less friends visit for dinner, perhaps to convince ourselves that we still have a social life. Our pals want to hear about my dubious effort to speak Italian to the boys, but mostly they want to chat about old times for hours. They don't understand we have dozens of pressing chores to do and rarely get a chance to rest unless it's to lie down to put a child to sleep.

Katy's friend Margaret is shocked we don't know about the latest local elections, commenting, "You guys really need to read more." Otto proceeds to spill his juice into the carpet and screams at his loss. Suddenly, Margaret understands why our evenings aren't spent perusing *The New Yorker* with our cat snuggled on our lap.

"All anyone really wants to do in life is sleep," I admit. Margaret looks at me amazed at how sleep-deprived we are. Eilif saves us from long evenings by approaching our guests lounging on the couch and announcing, unprompted, "Bye-bye! Bye-bye now!"

The boys scatter little toys like a minefield on the floor for any fool who dares to tread barefoot. Camouflaged into our colorful carpet, these booby traps inflict great pain on the toes of unwitting adults. I grew up with relatively few toys, but I refrain from criticizing the tsunami of knickknacks that enter our house. I too wanted toys galore when I was little, but I try to encourage gifts that will help us, such as books in Italian. No one listens.

Our parents bring over plastic key chains, colorful little bags, and other souvenirs they were about to throw away. They give them to the boys, who snatch up the knickknacks. Neighbors with grown kids donate dozens of grocery bags filled with not-so-gently-used toys. The boys want everything and stuff their bedrooms with worthless junk. One of Otto's fellow preschoolers fills his entire closet with trinkets and, as soon as he starts school, his mother throws out two trash bags full of his precious little gems. If our boys have their way, our bungalow will turn into a hoarder house.

Mostly, though, we let our boys keep their prized possessions, unless we know that they will hurt each other with them. When Eilif gets a pair of handcuffs as part of a cowboy costume, I see his eyes light up that he'll finally be able to control his pesky little preschool brother. When he's not looking, I snatch the handcuffs and hide them in our room.

Eilif doesn't notice, but Otto ventures into our room to snoop around for a secret stash of . . . well, anything. Otto finds the handcuffs and sneaks them across the street to play with little Grace, who is a few months younger than he is. Grace's mother, Annie, politely intercepts him and asks, "Say, Otto, where did you get those great handcuffs?"

"I found them in my parents' bedroom!" he reveals.

As the birthdays pile up, so do the gifts. Tickle-Me-Elmo's Let's Rock Guitar puts me over the edge. Katy agrees with me that this new demonic toy simply has no place in any home.

In the dark after Eilif's birthday party, I sneak into the living room and grab the insanity-inducing instrument. Only our cat Maggie notices me and, I imagine, approves of my plan. I throttle the guitar's neck and consider smashing it, Pete Townshend style. I balk, knowing that would wake the kids and they'd witness their psychotic father massacring their beloved new toy. I tiptoe to the trash and quietly slide the plastic guitar deep into a white Hefty bag. Elmo's giggle rings out; through coffee grounds, melted ice cream, and discarded birthday cake, the fretboard lights up the darkened room. The devilish muppet—the ghost in the machine—struggles for his life, calling out for help. I escape the scene of the crime.

The next morning before the kids wake, I walk into the kitchen to start the coffee. The floorboards creak, and the slightest motion triggers the tinny sounds of "Elmo's World" from deep within the kitchen waste. I quickly tie up the white trash sack as Elmo asks, "Do you want to be my friend?" I carry the blinking bag outside to the garbage cans as Elmo giggles menacingly and asks me if I want to play. Even as I walk away, the telltale heart calls for me. I return into the kitchen with a guilty look on my face, but Eilif doesn't notice Elmo's absence amid all the dinging and singing of his other electronic toys.

THE COST OF HAVING KIDS is adding up. We calculate how much day care costs, and we're losing money with Katy working part-time at the University of Minnesota. She decides to stay home with the two boys to cut costs by not working. Was it cheaper to live abroad in Italy?

When I talk to my parents about how exhausted we are, my dad responds, "You are so lucky."

What? I struggle to understand. But I recognize he's right. We have two adorable baby boys who are healthy, happy, and busy. Despite the overwhelming duty of providing and educating them, we must never forget they are our most important masterpieces.

My dad doesn't see it exactly that way, though, and gives me a copy of Kahlil Gibran's *The Prophet.* Inside is a poem: "Your children are not your children. . . . They come through you but not from you." He tells me that we must get to know our children because they are their own people. I think back to how my parents let me travel and discover who I am rather than tell me what to think. The book says, "You may give them your love but not your thoughts," but at least I can expose them to the world.

To do this, I translate their kids' books into Italian when I read them bedtime stories. Otto demands these distractions when he refuses to get his hair cut by Katy's friend at her salon in Dinkytown. She takes us downstairs in the barbershop into a closed-off basement room to prevent his howls from scaring away other customers. I sing him Italian songs, but still he wails. I try to distract him with frenetic, sugar-fueled modern cartoons in Italian, but that just ramps him up. Katy recites the book *Chicka Chicka Boom Boom* and shows him a Thomas the Tank Engine video. Finally he's calm. Did he just want to hear the English accent of narrator Ringo Starr?

Eilif watches the show intently and points out that "*La mamma* thinks she's just like Thomas the Tank Engine. No one works as hard as she does."

## HOW TO FIGHT A BEAR AT ITALIAN CAMP

To help our kids learn Italian during the summers, I take a job as the director of an overnight Italian camp. Kids from across the country come to a full-immersion camp; some of the staff and a few of the other campers are from Italy. The organization calls it a "language village" idealized as a mini version of Italy, except it's in the north woods of Minnesota, about as far away from southern Europe as possible.

How do I find counselors to work at an Italian camp in the middle of America? They must be close to fluent, good with children, and willing to sleep on a bunkbed in a cabin of up to ten people. Not only that, counselors must sing, act, and teach . . . all on the spur of the moment. I try to convince an Italian student at the University of Minnesota to apply to Italian camp, but she wonders, "Why would I want to spend my summer chasing kids when I can go to Italy?"

I emphasize to the staff that this isn't boot camp to learn Italian: We just need to show the kids how fun camp can be, all in Italian. I tell them how I want these kids, who risk it all to come to camp, to learn about the art, music, style, history, and food—in short, all the wonders of Italy. I ask them what

Italy means to them. Carlotta from Sicily says, "*Allegria!*" Joy and happiness.

My supervisor is so passionate about languages that it's alarming. In an article about polyglots, a national magazine featured my new boss who "started his day at three in the morning with a 'scriptorium' exercise: 'writing two pages apiece in Arabic, Sanskrit, and Chinese . . .' As dawn broke, he went for a long run listening to audiobooks . . . as the foreign sounds flowed into his headphones, he shouted them out at the top of his lungs." I tell the Italian counselors please not to do this, as it will frighten the children.

As our bus full of staff drives up from Minneapolis, the native Italians get nervous when a giant homemade sign along the highway demands: "Eat your meat and wear your furs. It's the American Way!"

Our nurse Coco points out that she doesn't eat beef, even if our cook Luca serves delicious meatballs with pork, beef, and raisins in tomato sauce.

"Why not?" Giovanni from Milano asks.

Coco explains, "I had a dream where this beautiful cow named Bessie came to me and after that, nope, no more beef for me."

"That's why we don't name our cows in Italy," Giovanni replies. "We just eat them."

"I used to eat meat, mostly chickens, since we raised them," Coco remembers. "Then our dog killed them all."

"You didn't eat the dog, did you?" Giovanni teases.

"No, but everyone was very upset."

Giovanni points out, "A dog like that wouldn't last long in Italy."

—

GERMAN CAMP
SAUVAGE!
O SOLE MIO
OUR PLANE
FRENCH CAMP
BEARS!
SERGIO
SAUNA
YUM! FROGS
CROW RISOTTO!
CHIPMUNKS
TWO
BUSES
ZETA'S BIKE IN TREE
"FRIENDLY" SOCCER
NINJA!
CHASING SKUNKS
PIAZZA
A SPY
THE BEACH
SHARK + OCTOPUS
PIRATES!
CAMP FIRES
CANOE IN TREE
CANOES
SHARKTOPUS!
RADIO
MY HOUSE
FISHING
VIA APPIA
IL
Campo
Italiano
VESPA
ALCESTE'S SPEEDO
CLINIC
ZOMBIES
HAPPY FISH
PONTE VECCHIO

Otto and Eilif are now just old enough to attend overnight camp, so I ask them who they think will make the best counselors. The boys tag along to orientation and try to figure out which of the counselors hail from Italy. They usually choose wrong. I point out the telltale sign is cool sunglasses. Alexandra and Nina, both from Torino, keep their sunglasses on during the canoe test of swamping the boats in the middle of the lake. They watch the rest of the counselors flip the boats and tread water as we scramble back inside the canoes. Alexandra and Nina don't see much point in this: "*Stiamo bene. Abbiamo capito come si fa!*" (We're fine. We understand how it's done.) They don't want to flap around in the water and, more importantly, they must make a *bella figura*, essentially look cool, at all costs.

Most of the counselors are cautious and restrained—except for Tiziana. Eilif adores her humor and wild side. He raves to Katy, "Tiziana is the coolest woman I know!" Katy seems a bit uneasy about Eilif's choice of a role model. He misreads her reaction and reassures her: "Oh, you're cool too, Mom, but Tiziana's cooler. I just wouldn't want her to be my mom."

Kids arrive at camp anxious at the prospect of spending weeks away from home. Being surrounded by a foreign language doesn't help calm their nerves, and for once Eilif and Otto's knowledge of Italian helps them fit in.

A ten-year-old girl, Francesca, is disappointed by Italian camp and confesses, "I expected Italian camp to be more like a spa."

Other new campers are unfazed by the natural surroundings and view their appearance at camp as a chance to make a splash. Fourteen-year-old Mirella steps out of her parents' car with an elegant sunhat that has an enormous brim shading her large sunglasses and waves of golden blonde hair. Her entrance might as well have been strutting down Via Veneto with Paparazzo's flashbulbs blazing and Marcello Mastroianni gazing at the scene. The mosquitoes don't faze her, and she doesn't need electricity in the cabins; she'd be classy even in a parka with blue jeans. She barely flinches when she gets a nosebleed and can't find a tissue. The blood drips from her nose and matches her cherry-red lipstick. Ever resourceful, she digs in her toiletries bag.

"Ciao Mirella," a cabinmate greets her, noticing the small plug in her nose with a string sticking out. "Is that . . . a . . . a tampon in your nose?"

"Yeah," Mirella replies. "I had a nosebleed, and it wouldn't stop." She is unconcerned about what anyone thinks of her.

Seeing Mirella and others let down their guard at camp helps new kids accept that they are in the forest far from home. Some, however, don't appreciate these "rustic" surroundings. The overwhelming metallic taste of the well water doesn't help; Eilif brags that it's "blood water." Some theorize that a camper got stuck in the well and bled to death. With each sip we take, we turn into vampires! Otto and Eilif are used to the iron in the water of northern Minnesota, but Francesca writes a worried letter to her parents, pleading, "Can you send me a bottle of water that doesn't smell like rotten eggs or taste like blood?"

The iron water lends a slight orange hue to the toilet bowls. Little Teodora is confused at first, but then informs her cabinmates, "The water in the toilet is already yellow, so you don't have to flush."

But not flushing leads to a ripe, stagnant smell with wads of toilet paper gathering in the bowl. When someone finally turns the handle to flush, disaster strikes. Fourteen-year-old Carmelo comes to the rescue. He later reflects on saving the day at that evening's cabin council that he's learned a new skill that shows both the high and low point of his day: "I plunged a toilet for the first time!" However, he still needs to learn to mop up the mess.

To prevent the camp from falling into filth and squalor, the nurse Coco tours the site each day to award the cleanest cabin prize. The female cabin of Lazio wins consistently, leading Otto to protest that "it's all rigged for the girls!"

I point out that a sour stench wafts from the boys' cabin, perhaps since they leave their wet towels and swimsuits to mold on the floor. It doesn't help their case when Filippo philosophizes, "My soap fell on the floor. Does that mean my soap is dirty or the floor is clean?" The boys question whether bathing is really so necessary if they will just get dirty again within a couple of hours.

The Italian counselor in Otto's cabin, used to immaculate Italian apartment living, won't put up with this. He inspires the boys to win the cleanest cabin award for almost an entire week. The girls now complain that it's all rigged for the boys since boys can't possibly be cleaner than girls.

I TELL THE STAFF that the main reason for these kids to take showers, sweat in the sauna, or go swimming is to cleanse their bodies of chemicals. Every day, the boys in Otto's cabin soak their bodies with a glistening layer of Deep Woods Off. Despite our best efforts to stop them, they sometimes shut their eyes and spray toward their faces. I've seen them protect their eyes from the spray by wearing sunglasses but then wipe off the insect repellent on their towels, which they rub over their bodies and throw on the floor. Even if the mosquitoes aren't so bad, the kids will do anything to avoid being bitten.

One day when I'm walking by the little girls' cabin of Emilia-Romagna, I hear a scream: "An ant! There's an ant!" Some of them run outside until the mini monster vanishes. After a lot of stomping, presumably to smash the ant or climb into the bunks, the terror stops. I don't dare tell them about the spiders in the eaves who are busy catching mosquitoes.

In Otto's cabin, the little boys try to act tough about nature. Little Samuele mocks his skittish cabinmates: "Don't tell me you're afraid of bugs!"

"Yeah! Especially if they're big bugs," responds Luigi. "I'm afraid of anything that moves!"

"That's ridiculous," Samuele scoffs. "Then you're even afraid of yourself!"

Antonio calms down Luigi: "North Korea may have nukes, but we have 98 percent DEET, so I'm not worried."

Rather than leaving the insects alone, the younger boys take matters into their own hands. They talk loudly and carry a big stick. We warn them that with a big stick comes big responsibility, especially when furious bees seek revenge.

One day we can't find Otto and Gianfrancesco, who should be in their language group. I hike all over camp looking for them only to find them smashing a rotting stump with sticks. Hundreds of confused ants crawl willy-nilly over the decomposing wood. As Gianfrancesco takes another swing, he tells me, "*Questo è fantastico! Mi piace la natura.*" (This is fantastic! I like nature.)

—

NATURE IS NOT JUST A PROBLEM for the campers. At our staff meeting, the nurse Coco shows me a plastic bag filled with bear scat she found on the path. Two of the counselors say that they saw the same kind of poop a few days before and just moved it off the path. The caretaker tells me that he heard a mamma bear and her two cubs were spotted on the other side of the soccer field.

We try to assure the native Italian staff that these are black bears, not grizzlies, and are rarely dangerous to humans. Regardless, a counselor from Wisconsin totes her bear spray that sprays up to forty feet. At the same time, she would never hurt a fly and shows us photos of a cute bear at her bird feeder back home in northern Wisconsin.

We keep the bear spray safely stashed, as I imagine someone accidentally spraying a deer, a raccoon, or—worse—a camper. A counselor from Alaska claims to know bears better than anyone. "If it's brown, lay down! If it's black, fight back! If the bear doesn't run when you make noise, just conk them on the nose," he declares so convincingly that we all believe him. "If they open their mouth, you jam your fist down their throat."

One of the Italians asks what we do if we see an *orso polare*, or polar bear.

"If it's white, say good night!" he proclaims, as the Italians panic.

The next day, the counselor Lupo takes the campers to the archery range up the road. One of the campers recognizes fresh bear scat near the targets. Lupo tells the campers that they should just return quietly to the main buildings, "and perhaps it's best we don't tell anyone else since we don't want them to get upset. Besides, we didn't actually *see* the bear."

As soon as they return to the cabin, one of them announces to the boys in Otto's cabin, "Guess what? We saw bear poop! There are bears out in the woods ready to eat us!" A camper gets himself so worked up that he vomits on the shoes of the boy who spread the news.

"Did we learn our lesson?" Lupo asks. "See, this is why we didn't want others to panic."

LITTLE BY LITTLE, the kids grow to appreciate nature, even if the red squirrels drop acorns on the roofs of the cabins and a raccoon tips over the garbage cans *every* night.

Some of the campers think wild animals are like fuzzy pets waiting to be cuddled. In the camp store, I see a group of four campers cornering a "cute little chipmunk." They take pictures, and a girl leans down to pet and snuggle "the little guy."

"Stop!" I yell, breaking the language barrier.

They step back surprised but chide me: "You're supposed to say it in Italian!" The chipmunk escapes, and I avoid having to dislodge a scared rodent from the girl's face.

A COUPLE OF THE BOYS at Italian camp capture toads hopping around and show them to the girls.

Little Alessandra is disgusted: "Eww! Frogs are sticky and gross!"

"So are children," the counselor Vale points out.

Even so, the kids admire the six loons in the swimming area with the baby loon hiding in the weeds. They notice the beavers slowly swimming near the shore by the huge muskie getting warm in the shallow water. They realize the majesty of a bald eagle perching on a dead branch above our heads searching for dinner.

We never see the bear. Mostly, we're relieved that we have the same number of campers at the beginning and end of the summer. No more, no less. The long goodbyes drag on as the kids exchange contact information and the bus driver impatiently points to her watch. The campers cry when they arrive and cry when they leave.

Once the boys get home, Katy is exasperated that Eilif has somehow lost two towels and a swimsuit at camp. "That's all?" he questions proudly. "Aren't you proud of me, mom?"

# JESUS CAT

I browse through brochures and dream about our possible lives in Italy. Where should we live? Rome? Back in Modena? We can barely afford to live in Minneapolis, so I take a full-time position teaching at a university. I convince myself that rather than keeping us in the United States, this job will create opportunities to teach abroad in Italy.

Meanwhile, Katy insists we get a dog. I refuse, as we have our hands full with two kids and a cat. She won't listen. Already a cat could hinder us from living in Italy; a dog could stop us altogether. That's not the discussion, however, as every conversation seems to revolve around what kind of dog we should get, how beneficial a dog is for the kids, how the dog will protect the kids and the house, and just how darn cute puppies are. She convinces the boys too, and they all promise—promise!—to take care of the dog and clean up after it.

I continue to resist, but Katy doesn't back down. She wonders why I'm such a "dog hater" and starts questioning my character and if we're really made for each other. When my brother, who lives two blocks away, announces that he's going to get a Bernese mountain dog, Katy says that is the final straw. We simply must get a dog. A black-and-white Australian shepherd joins our family. We name him "Bacco," Italian for Bacchus, because of his constant indulgence.

Our mean cat Maggie hates Bacco, whose dopey good nature wins me over. All the cuteness of a new puppy doesn't work on Eilif. He's glum and going through an existential crisis at six years old. Our inevitable mortality hits him hard. He realizes that not paying attention while walking across the street could be the end of his life. Every departure could be the last time we see each other. When I go out of town for a few days for work, his little brother Otto assures me, "Papà, you're really going to miss us!"—*not* "I'm going to miss you."

Eilif says to Katy, "Mamma, I just hope we don't die while Papà is gone."

Soon everything is related to death. Eilif accidentally hurts himself in kindergarten with a pencil and complains to his teacher, "I don't think I'm going to make it until I'm ten. I'm going to die because all my skin is going to fall off!"

His classmate Daria tries to console him, "Well, Eilif, if you die, at least we'll all miss you!"

Either Eilif is truly upset he's not invincible or he's manipulating us for pity. One night at dinner when he refuses to eat his vegetables, he gets up from the table and declares, "I'm going outside to freeze to death. I'm going outside to go to heaven." He stands outside in the snow for a bit, pouts, and then comes back inside to warm up. His angst has passed.

We hope this is a phase, but how do we explain our morbid little kindergartner? When it's time to leave a birthday party, he melts down. Rather than saying "thank you" to the hosts, he shouts, "Bye everybody! Thanks for the party! I'm going to get run over by a car now."

After a month, he isn't quite so preoccupied with his imminent demise. "I'm not so worried about dying anymore because my name 'Eilif' means 'immortal,'" he tells me. He realizes that perhaps there's an upside to all this death business. He asks Katy, "Mamma, can I have the iPad when you and Papà die?"

Exasperated, Katy sighs, "Sure, Eilif. You can have the iPad when we die."

"Yes!" He pumps his fist in the air.

"No way! That's not fair," Otto complains. "What do I get?"

KATY EXPLAINS Eilif's *Harold and Maude* moments to her friend, a naturopath, who recommends church so Eilif has a place to ask these existential questions. Katy is skeptical, describing herself as "a recovering Catholic" who can never quite free herself from the clutches of the Church. How can she ever escape the pope after living in Italy for two years and being sent to Catholic schools all her life?

Katy proclaims, "I like religion. I do!"

"Really?" I ask. "Since when?"

Katy thinks a bit. "No, I suppose I don't like religion . . . but I do want our kids to have a relationship with God. I just want it to be consensual and mutually respectful, like any relationship."

We search for a church. I grew up in a liberal Presbyterian church where the minister had just run off with the music director and we sang "Kumbaya" with gusto. Katy nixed that church. We thought a Unitarian church might fit our beliefs, but my brother told me about a Universalist minister in southern Minnesota who declared, "Praise be to God . . . if there is one." The Unitarian church in Minneapolis features reckless kids on skateboards and earsplitting whistles for the Christmas pageant. That's not great, but the last straw for Katy is a meditation bell signaling three minutes of silence—an impossibility with little boys.

Katy considers the Buddhist temple, but our Italian friend Guido informs us that everyone just spends their time wishing for things by chanting *nam-myoho-renge-kyo.* "There were lots of cute girls," Guido remembers, "but who wants to be around all that chanting?"

Eventually, we give in to the Catholic pull that has a hold on Katy, as the fear of a reprimand for an incorrect genuflection still lives strong in her. We end up at the Basilica of Saint Mary in Minneapolis, and the boys join the choir. Otto, however, refuses to perform in public unless I'm standing next to him. I end up holding his hand and singing with the choir in front of the packed church for both Christmas and Easter as Katy smirks at me from the front pews. She says there's no way she would get up there.

I hope the baroque, beaux-arts Basilica will give the boys a glimpse of the grandeur of Italian churches that we'll someday see in Rome. The incense spiraling up to the gilded ceiling turns all shades of the rainbow as the light shining through the stained-glass windows illuminates the smoke like a kaleidoscopic ghost. Our two wild boys relax under the tall ceilings held up by enormous marble columns. Otto loves the beauty but is bored. At the end of the service, he draws upon his experience attending plays and cheers, "Hurray! The show's over! We get to go home!"

On those mornings when we make it to church, Katy and I get a break from the boys while they attend Sunday school. As the priest drones on about the birth of Jesus and how kings came from far and wide to worship the baby, Katy whispers to me, "Good Lord! What would Mary have done with a kid like Jesus who thinks he's God? How do you deal with that?"

When the boys return to the pews after Sunday school, I worry what sort of answers they'll hear about life's persistent questions. Surprisingly, Eilif had a great time. He took photocopies of Jesus and the saints that the teacher handed out and drew capes and masks on them to turn them into invincible superheroes with special powers. At the end of mass, he approaches the priest walking down from the altar and is awed by his outfit. "Cool cape!" he calls to him.

Otto looks at Eilif's drawings and asks me in Italian, "Papà, do you know God and Jesus?"

"Umm, a little, I guess," I answer nervously, but want to find out what he's learned: "What do they do?"

"They play," Otto responds.

Eilif is clearly concerned his little brother has learned nothing, so he quizzes him, "What else?"

"They eat pizza and go to school," Otto adds.

Eilif asks Katy, "Who is God's wife?"

Katy is stumped, but Eilif presses on asking about baby Jesus. Katy knows this one: "He's the son of God."

"And his mamma is Mary and father is Joseph," continues Eilif proudly.

"Yes," she confirms.

Eilif calculates, "God is Mary's husband and Joseph is Jesus's daddy, so Jesus has two daddies!"

WHEN EASTERTIME ARRIVES at the Basilica, Katy explains to the boys that on Palm Sunday we wave palm fronds as a symbol of victory for Jesus when he entered Jerusalem. I tell them, "They still waved the palm fronds in Italy when we were there."

"Why?" asks Otto. "Didn't they have flags?"

In Sunday school, the boys learn how to fold palm fronds into crosses. Eilif and Otto recognize that a cross is the same shape as a sword and a duel begins.

The discussion of Easter inevitably leads back to death. One evening while brushing his teeth, Eilif proclaims, "When I die, I want to be buried in a box."

"I don't," Otto responded. "When I die, I want to be Jesus."

"Why?" I ask.

"Well, he came back from the dead," Otto reasons, "kind of like a zombie."

Eilif concludes, "So we worship a zombie? Cool."

The obsession with death subsides until a baby is born down the block. Eilif is upset by the news. "What's wrong?" Otto asks.

Eilif enlightens his brother, "Each time a baby is born, someone else has to die."

Katy explains that we can celebrate this new birth because there is no set number of people who can be alive. Eilif scoffs at how naïve she is.

Otto, however, has learned not to take the advice of his brother too seriously. He is not disturbed, as I expected, upon discovering that the meat on the dining room table was once a living creature. We go through the various animals: Pork comes from pigs, beef is from cows, venison is deer . . . In fact, Otto is thrilled by this revelation and tells his brother, "Hey Eilif, when animals die, they become food! Dogs become 'hot dogs.' Mamma, what kind of food are cats when they die?"

—

We have cat problems. Eilif and Otto repeatedly try to pet Maggie, our furry little beast who sleeps in sunbeams. She lashes out, leaving them with scratches and crocodile tears. How can such a cute kitty be so cruel? Katy and I reason she is just wary of kids eager to pull her tail, but she claws them even when they are gentle. No matter how much we dote on her, she bats at us. Even our bold dog Bacco is terrified of her and pees whenever she comes after him. He won't descend into the basement where she sleeps. Katy and I wonder: Why are we supporting a cat who hates us?

This past year Maggie has constantly missed her litter box, and our hungry dog gobbles up the little "treats" she leaves around the house. For a year, Katy tries herbal remedies with no luck, and the vet agrees that poor Maggie must be very sick. The vet helps us make the decision to put Maggie to sleep: "Your cat knows what her job is, and she isn't doing it." With that reasoning, however, we figure we could be free of some of the other little creatures in our house.

Eilif and Otto gush with grief. Maggie hides in the basement because of all the wailing. The boys don't even look for her, which is better because she would just scratch them. I track her down and load her into the pet carrier as the boys cry their sad goodbyes through the bars of the cage. Maggie tries to bite and claw them.

With the grim duty of executioner, I sit at the vet's reception area on death row. Across from me, two women in pink and purple dresses spread out over two plastic chairs. "Is that a wittle puddy tat?" coos the lady with pigtails. She wiggles her finger outside the cat cage and fusses, "Gootchie gootchie!" Maggie hisses violently in response. Their Pomeranian-Maltese dog named "Sweetheart" wears a pink knit sweater with glittery hearts all over it and piddles on the welcome mat. One of the vets dutifully sops it up with a towel.

Sweetheart finds me, even though I want to be left alone, and humps my shoe enthusiastically. "Sweetheart likes you! Isn't that nice?" As I struggle to free myself from the surprisingly tight grip of the lusty pup, I consider pulling Maggie out of the cage for one last hurrah.

I ARRIVE HOME with an empty cage, and the situation hasn't improved. Katy has lit candles to calm the kids—as a sort of wake for Maggie. With tears running down his face, Eilif declares, "If she can't live, I don't want to live!" He then has a revelation: "She died so we could be free!" He now considers her "Wonder Cat," but then changes his mind. "No, she's more than that. She's Jesus Cat!" This, of course, turns Katy and me into Judas Iscariot and Pontius Pilate.

The next day, Eilif tells his teacher he wants to write a book about Maggie's life. "Is five pages enough?" his teacher asks.

"No, I need at least ten." Although he considers her "Jesus Cat," he can't decide whether to title her biography "Mean Cat" or "Cat Attack."

The teacher lets Eilif mourn by spending the day drawing his dead cat. The story centers around Eilif dressing up in superhero outfits and crushing villains.

"How's it going with your dead cat?" asks his classmate Eliza. Eilif is too choked up to respond. "We had the same problem," she confides, "but I learned that if you lift up its tail and the tail stays up, it's alive. If it stays down, it's dead."

Since the boys are so moved by their mean cat, we pay to have Maggie cremated. By the time the ashes arrive weeks later, the boys have lost interest. The dog is still terrified of the basement, but our lives are instantly easier. We have more free time because we no longer have to clean up after the cat each morning. Eilif was right: She died so we could be free . . . and maybe even to go to Italy.

## KILLING KIDS WITH HAMBURGERS

Education choices plague us. Should we send our kids to a language immersion school, even if none of the schools teach Italian? Should we homeschool our kids, despite desperately wanting a break from them? We wonder if the supposed "tiger moms" are on to something by thrusting their offspring to higher heights. One of the counselors from Italian camp went to teach at a school in South Korea that pushed kids to perfection, or at least to conform. She tells me that a school administrator advised her that to make her pupils behave, "We've stopped hitting kids as of this year, but you can still put them in the corner and make them hold their arms in the air for the rest of the day."

Some Francophiles rave about the French manner of raising their *bébés*: Treat them as little adults, do not dote on them, and even ignore them so they figure out their own way. A fellow parent toured a private French school in Minneapolis and asked what sets it apart from the public schools. "Rigor!" the principal exclaimed and wiggled her index finger strictly.

When I was five and my family lived in Belgium, I went to a French-speaking public school. The ruthless nuns made sure we kindergarteners didn't put our elbows on the table at lunch. The nuns corrected us with a little slap to the back of the head. Disobedient children in the classroom spent time in the closet. On the playground, the naughtiest boys got tied to a tree until the end of recess while other kids taunted them.

Fortunately my parents pulled me from that school and enrolled me in a Belgian hippie school called Le Verseau, named for the Age of Aquarius. The school nurtured kids with nature, animals (including a lion), and insisted we write with both hands to be ambidextrous. We ate food that we grew in the garden and didn't get slapped for table manners. The school cultivated wholistic kids with lots of music and art. Unfortunately, we don't live in Belgium now.

I attempt to bring that atmosphere home to teach the kids to learn to cook and to grow our own herbs and vegetables. Regardless, our food has no flavor as the kids don't like spice. Only the blandest food pleases their palates. I make rich pasta or risotto dishes to prepare them to go to Italy. The kids poke at the food with their forks and won't even taste it. I finally get them to eat *cotoletta alla milanese* with lemons and *pasta al pesto genovese.*

Even though Eilif and Otto are picky eaters, I want them to try food from all over the world, not just Italy. I tell Katy about a trip my doctor took to Belgium, where she saw little kids asking for more herring. "Can't we be like that?" I say. "I don't want to be one of those families that eat just wieners and mac and cheese."

"Yeah, good luck with that," Katy quips.

I remind Katy of her dad's advice: "If I've learned one thing, the kids won't let themselves go hungry and will eventually eat." Katy isn't convinced.

I prepare a batch of Swiss cheese fondue, considering it "fun food." The boys are fascinated by the dangerous flame at the table that could potentially burn down the house. We stop the inevitable sword fight with the long, sharp forks and encourage them to stab their bread instead of each other. Eilif cautiously dips his chunk of crusty French bread into the bubbling hot cheese and blows on it to cool it off. He pops it into his mouth and looks at me as if I've betrayed his trust. How could I do this to him? He spits everything out and wipes his tongue off with his hand and then his napkin. He cries at the outrage of this disgusting food and then makes himself a peanut butter and jam sandwich.

The boys wonder whether I'm trying to poison them with my bizarre food. They trust Bacco the dog more. He becomes their loyal food taster, licking their food before they put it in their mouths.

As the boys remain suspicious of my motives, they soon trust each other's tastes and share their food. I push them not to eat in the car, but Katy views this as a losing battle, especially when we take a two-week road trip through Wisconsin.

In a gritty part of Green Bay, we stop for gas. I tell the boys to leave their food in the car, but Otto insists on carrying his cookie into the filthy gas station restroom. As he's pulling down his pants to sit on the potty, he drops his precious ginger snap onto the wet floor. I try to grab it and toss it in the trash before he notices. He cries for his cookie as I assure him that we can get another in the car.

Eilif, the big-hearted brother, reaches into the garbage can and pulls out the moist cookie and hands it to Otto, who says, "Thank you, Eilif!" As I try to snatch the sweets again, the gas station attendant with neck tattoos and a Mack truck baseball cap shakes his head at what a cruel father I am.

As a reward for trying different kinds of food, we let the boys choose the food on their birthdays. "For breakfast I want corn dogs," Otto announces.

"Really? Corn dogs? Have you ever even had one?" Katy asks.

"Well, no, but they look so good," Otto replies. Thankfully he is satisfied when she suggests caramel rolls instead.

Eilif, on the other hand, begs us to go to McDonald's. Even if we don't want them to become fast-food addicts, we let him order three hamburgers, which he puts away readily.

Katy asks, "When you're grown up and live on your own, is that all you'll eat?"

"Yeah, then you'll weigh eight hundred pounds!" Otto warns.

"That will be fine," Eilif responds seriously. "If I weigh eight hundred pounds, I won't have to wear a jacket because I'll never get cold."

Then a nutrition course at Eilif's school sponsored by the local co-op strikes fear in the little boy. He is suddenly terrified that the food we serve will kill him. For my part, I worry that our boys are skinnier than ever. To fatten them up, I grill giant hamburgers. Otto grabs one hungrily.

"If I eat one, I'll die of a heart attack!" Eilif wails.

"That's if you eat fast-food hamburgers all the time," Katy explains.

"Mmm, it's yummy," Otto mumbles with his mouth full. "Eilif, you should try it."

Eilif cries into his hands, "You're all trying to kill me! Why are you doing this to me?"

"What do you mean?" I reply. "You ate three McDonald's hamburgers the other day, and this is good, organic beef."

Eilif refuses to touch it and runs screaming to his bedroom.

Otto finishes off his one-third-pound hamburger and takes advantage of the situation to eat Eilif's burger as well.

Through a mixture of rewards, cajoling, and old-fashioned fearmongering, the boys slowly experiment with different kinds of food. We adopt my Swedish grandmother's propaganda of pushing us to become members of the "clean plate club." Then at seven they even become members of the "salad club."

They do expand their palate, which we learn when Eilif goes to a week of Norwegian overnight camp. "Mamma, I've changed," he declares when he comes home. "I really have! I'm very different now. I like plums. I never knew I liked plums. I like Diet Coke too."

"Yeah, but each time you drink it, you have to spit it out because of all the fizz so it doesn't come out your nose," Otto reminds him.

"At least I'm eating different things, Otto!"

## THE BIRTH OF VENUS

"At home? You want to give birth at home?" I'm in disbelief as Katy informs me that our third child will be born in our dining room. I argue that perhaps we should quickly move over to Europe to have the government health care cover the costs. I had laid out plans to bring us back to Italy, but now we won't be able to go for a few more years. What's more, I may have to deliver the baby myself.

I suppose it makes sense that Katy wants to give birth in her own space rather than in an antiseptic hospital with male doctors running the show. "Besides," she adds, "the doctors always push patients to do extra procedures." She wants this process to be as natural as possible.

I argue in vain that giving birth at home is what our great-grandparents did a century ago. "Exactly," she exclaims. "We need to get back to basics."

A GRINNING BUDDHA STATUE greets us as we enter a midwife's house and remove our shoes. The midwife, who also teaches prenatal yoga, offers us herbal tea as the boys sit on cushions and play with wooden blocks. The midwife puts an ear trumpet to Katy's belly.

I express my hesitation about a home birth, but she shushes me. "We're listening for the baby's heartbeat."

I wait. Then I blurt out, "I just don't want to deliver the baby myself!"

"Well, we've never missed a placenta," the midwife laughs.

The placenta comes about twenty minutes after the baby's birth. "What do you mean?" I stutter.

"We'll be just fine," Katy assures me.

"No need to worry," the midwife confirms. "We're only fifteen minutes away."

BACK HOME, Katy shows Eilif and Otto some children's biology books that explain in graphic detail the origin of babies. Otto memorizes the technical terms—"fallopian tubes," and so on. Eilif is unconvinced by this scientific mumbo jumbo. He wants to go back further in time. "So when did this whole world get started?"

Otto realizes his brother is on to something. "Yeah, when did this world get built, anyway?" As if Katy and I have been concealing secrets from them.

I explain about the early volcanic earth, dinosaurs, and the evolution of mammals. They're unconvinced. Just then the five-year-old neighbor girl Grace knocks on the door. Eilif grills her, "Do you know where you come from?"

Otto repeats the interrogation: "Yeah, Grace, where did you come from?"

Grace points innocently, "I came from my house across the street."

Eilif scoffs, "No, Grace, where did you *really* come from?"

At the first ultrasound, the nurse rubs gel on Katy's belly, and we hear the heartbeat. The nurse tells us, "It looks like both of them are doing great!"

"Both? What do you mean?"

"You didn't know they are twins?" she asks.

Four kids? We struggle to understand what this means. We will be outnumbered two to one!

At the next ultrasound, though, the nurse only finds one fetus. "It's actually quite common and probably happens much more than we realize," she reassures us. In the old days, no one knew about the "silent twin" disappearing early in pregnancy. Regardless, we mourn the idea of missing this fourth child that we were just beginning to imagine.

The midwife warns us that babies come in bunches, so they might be busy when Katy's water breaks. "Luckily there are two of us, so one should be able to break free," the midwife tells me as she hauls a birthing tub into our house. A thrilled Otto is ready to put on his swim trunks to jump into our new indoor pool, or "birth pond."

As we prepare for the insanity of three kids under the age of eight in our house, we remember the advice of our Italian adopted grandmother: "*Chi ha un porco solo lo fa grasso, e chi ha un figlio solo lo fa matto,*" or "Whoever has just one pig will make it fat, and whoever has just one child will make him crazy." In other words, we need more than one child so they aren't spoiled. The grandmother assures us that "one child isn't enough and two is too many!" I'm not sure what that makes three . . . perhaps insanity.

We don't know the gender of the baby; Otto is worried a baby brother will take his toys.

To brainwash Eilif and Otto, we refer to their impending new sibling as "your baby." Katy prepares for the baby's birthday party by getting soda pop, chips, and a new children's video that they can watch. Katy wants the boys to be home during the birth.

"Really? Don't you think that will be a little much for them?" I respond. She tells me that it's our society that has made birth into such a clinical, disgusting act. She sits with the boys and pages through her books, allowing them to put their hands on her belly to feel "their" baby.

Katy's water breaks at 9 a.m. The boys are thrilled; I'm not so calm. I call up the midwife and tell her what's happening.

"Do you think you want a midwife now?" she asks calmly.

Is this sarcasm? I don't want to panic because I know the process can take a while. Still, Katy's last delivery was quick, within a few hours of her water breaking. "Umm . . . I think that would be a good idea."

The midwife obviously doesn't want to rush over only to wait. "Why don't you see how Katy's doing now, and we'll chat in a little while. Bye!"

This is not good. Katy is calm but wants everything ready. I bus our breakfast dishes, move aside the table, and lay out the pool. The air pump screeches and wheezes while Katy complains she just wants peace and quiet. She sets up the boys in another room with a video and mounds of snack food.

I screw an elaborate brass plumbing contraption onto our kitchen spigot to feed water through a garden hose into the moaning pool taking shape in our dining room. This pool will weigh a couple thousand pounds, and I worry our ninety-year-old Scotch pine joists could crumble.

Katy asks me to shut our blinds. I wonder if other incidents like this are taking place behind the curtains in the other houses down the block.

Lost in my thoughts, I see Katy's face in pain from contractions. I call the midwife again, but she's not convinced it's time. I don't want to deliver this baby myself.

She finally shows up. Katy is holding her belly and breathing deeply. The midwife measures to see if Katy has dilated. "Wow, this baby is coming soon!" For once I feel vindicated.

The midwife springs into action. Katy doesn't like the noise and wants to take a walk. "What do you mean?" I panic.

Katy explains, "I just need time to think."

"Now?"

The midwife tells me that walking will help lower the baby into the birth canal. "Can't you just walk around the house?" I ask. Katy opens the door and walks down the street alone.

I'm shocked. I thought she was going to give birth, and now we're taking a stroll? I run out to catch up to her. Will I have to deliver the baby on a neighbor's lawn? She has slowed to a waddle as the baby is probably poking through her legs.

A few blocks away, she says, "OK, I'm ready now. Let's go have this baby!"

We walk arm-in-arm as ever-more painful contractions slow her down.

We barely make it back home. Katy steps into the warm water of the birthing pool in the same room we had breakfast not long ago. In twenty minutes, she's fully dilated. "Get the kids!" she tells me. I interrupt their *Phineas and Ferb* cartoon. By the time we return, the infant's bluish head is poking out underwater. Katy shouts, "No, wait. Not yet. Keep the boys away!" She wants to avoid potentially traumatizing them.

I watch this miracle of our beautiful infant coming into the world.

The midwife expertly catches the baby underwater. She dries off the newborn with warm towels and hands the newborn to Katy.

"It's a girl!" the midwife declares. Katy cuddles the baby, and her heartbeat soothes the infant. Finally, Katy can rest. She mentions that it's like the birth of Venus from the foam of the sea.

We try out different names. I want "Inger," since "Inger Dregni" is a palindrome. We agree on "Astri," a little Norwegian star.

"Is she going to stay so purple and red?" Otto wonders.

Eilif points to her. "Look! Her head is like a cone!"

The boys notice the umbilical cord and seem worried that the baby will stay attached to their mother. The midwife clamps two tongs on the long, dark tube connecting their new little sister to her mother. She asks the boys if they would like to cut the cord, but they're nervous of blood spouting everywhere. I take the scissors and cut the bond.

THE MIDWIFE DELIVERS the placenta as promised. Afterward, she shows everyone how the lines on the placenta form a pattern of an expanding tree, much like our growing family.

The steel bowl that holds the placenta has some red fluid left in it. Eilif is intrigued. "Is that blood?" he asks.

"Yes," she replies, pleased that he's taken some interest.

"Is that *real* blood?"

"Yes, it is."

"Can I have it?" Eilif asks. "I want to do something creepy with it."

"We'll have to ask your mother later," she responds, unfazed.

After Katy has rested, the midwife asks her what she wants to do with her placenta. She explains that some cultures bury the placenta and plant a tree over it. Some grind up the placenta and put it into capsules to eat because of all the nutrients that this restores to the mother's body. Katy hesitates but agrees to eat her placenta . . . later.

The next week, the midwife drops off a plastic bag filled with vegetable capsules stuffed with fresh placenta that could easily be confused with any vitamin. Katy is clearly disturbed by her commitment to eat one of her organs. Is this cannibalism? But aren't you a cannibal only if you eat someone else? What if you eat yourself? The capsules remain untouched in the freezer.

A NEW SISTER is an educational experience. Otto has studied his biology book and watches the baby breastfeed. "I see how Astri drinks," he observes, "but how does she eat?"

Katy explains that she gets her food through the breast too. Otto is impressed. "Wow, those are some pretty cool breasts you got there!"

Eilif concurs. "Women are lucky that they have big milk containers that they carry with them wherever they go."

Little Astri also provides comedy, as poopy diapers are very funny. They plug their noses, pretend to gag, and laugh hysterically when I change her pants. Otto realizes that Astri doesn't have a little penis like he does. "Hey Eilif, look! Astri has *two* butts!"

"Wow, cool!"

I explain that they once pooped their pants too. They are embarrassed, and my reminder deters the endless repetition of "poopy pants."

Fortunately, the two big brothers don't see this fresh addition as competition. They are smitten. "Papà, you know who I want to marry when I grow up?" Otto asks. "I want to marry Astri."

# LEARN TO ARGUE LIKE AN ITALIAN

My stoic Scandinavian, German, and British background taught me that anyone who gets upset, raises their voice, and argues is, by definition, wrong. When I was an exchange student in northern Italy in high school, I saw the light. Arguing is an art, one accompanied by colorful gestures. This is passion. Standing in the piazza with your friends (and enemies) to discuss the news or even just the weather is exhilarating and confrontational rather than monotone conformity and boring agreement. I wanted our kids to learn how to interact without staring at their shoes and dare to challenge someone who says it's a nice day.

My high school classmates in Brescia taught me all the *parolacce*, or swear words. My classmate Marco proudly made an entire list of *bestemmie*, or blasphemies, against God, the saints, the Virgin Mary, and anyone else he could think of. Now my university students want to learn all the bad words and accompanying gestures in Italian, but I hesitate teaching them since I know this is all they'll remember. Still, these are important words and gestures to know if someone is doing them to you.

With our boys, I wonder if we should mimic the Italian school system that I experienced and make our kids memorize pages from law, economics, accountancy books, and Dante. They could learn Greek, Latin, and all the Western classics. My Italian teachers in high school gave surprise "oral interrogations" in front of the whole class, and all grades were posted to humiliate everyone equally. The Italian system didn't ask for students to evaluate the teachers, who were often hated but mostly feared and therefore "respected" in the best Machiavellian tradition.

I reconsider the Italian way after hearing the experience of our friend who taught in Sardegna for a year. She tells us, "The students regularly argue with the teachers about when they should take their oral exams." Once a teacher yelled at a student for twenty minutes in front of the whole class. Afterward, our friend told the teacher that she felt uncomfortable with this approach, to which the teacher responded, "Sooner or later, it had to be done," as if yelling at kids helps them learn. The student failed anyway.

Slowly, the boys are understanding more Italian, but they just think it's an odd language their papà speaks. One of the teachers at the boys' school is excited about Italian and tells me, "I'm planning on going to Italy and want to learn the language!" I tell her that she should talk to the boys because she sees them every day. "I tried," she says, "but Otto told me, 'Umm, you should just talk to my dad.'"

Eilif and Otto clearly need to see that other people speak Italian besides me. We sign them up for Italian lessons at the Italian Cultural Center in downtown Minneapolis, where a group of other bilingual kids get together on Saturday mornings. My hopes were dashed by the realization that all these

Italian kids just get together and teach each other the worst swear words in Italian.

One Saturday evening, Eilif wants to demonstrate that he can keep it clean. He proves to us that he can be a perfect boy. For him this means policing his little brother. He monitors Otto's every word. In a panic, Eilif reports to me, "Papà! Otto just said the P word!"

Hmmm. I wonder what the "P word" is?

Eilif warns again. "That's a really bad word, Otto!"

"It is?"

"Yeah. You better look out! There's the A word, the B word, the C word, the D word. All the way to the Z word."

"What's the Z word?" Otto asks.

"I don't know, but I bet it's pretty bad!" Eilif says.

Rather than actually cussing, the first letter becomes synonymous for that deviant word, but we often don't know what they're talking about. During a parent–teacher conference, Katy asks Eilif's first-grade teacher: "What exactly is the 'B word'?"

"You don't know what the B word is?" the teacher asks in disbelief, as if Katy has been too protected.

"Well, I just don't know what *they* think it is."

Once the mysterious B word is revealed, the teacher proceeds to tell Katy a story about the "F word." A mother and daughter were waiting in line at Dairy Queen on Lake Street. The daughter overheard an argument between a man at the front of the line and the poor cashier serving ice cream. "Can you believe that?" the daughter emphatically said to the distracted mom. "He just called her the F word!"

The shocked mother replied, "He really said that?"

"Yeah, he called her fat!" the daughter exclaimed.

The mother agreed, "That is bad!"

—

NOW THAT BABY ASTRI has joined the scrum, I ask Eilif and Otto if they can speak only Italian with her so she'll be bilingual. "*Certo!*" they assure me and start speaking English to her. They seem incapable. Everything we do seems to fail.

"How on earth did we get to be parents?" Katy asks. "We're not qualified. You should have to have a good job, a full bank account, and lessons. To drive a car, you need a license; to do any job there are years of schooling. The most important job—raising a human being—requires no training."

She deduces that Eilif must have an "auditory response problem."

I ask, "You mean that he just doesn't listen?"

"Exactly!"

I suggest that perhaps the boys have "selective listening" and only hear what they want. We consider that I should just stop speaking Italian to them since they often choose not to listen. We resolve to try to keep up the bilingual game when we realize they're just pretending to not understand.

I explain to Eilif, who was watching this scene, that not everything at our house is "fair." Katy and I are the parents, and they are the children. We are not equals. I consider Italian history and tell him about the hierarchy in the city-states. "It's a little like we are the king and the queen," I add stupidly.

"Then we're just servants?" Eilif cries.

"No, servants actually work, and you do very little," I say, using a terrible metaphor of monarchs and serfs. I shift the comparison and explain that Katy and I are like trainers of Pokémon creatures. Eilif, Otto, and Astri are little Pokémon who we want to evolve.

Suddenly, this all makes sense to Eilif. "That's great!" He smiles. "So we need to do our job to level up. I get it."

Otto, on the other hand, is turning my own trick on me. When they respond to me in English, I repeat in Italian what I wanted their answer to be. Instead of asking me something, Otto almost seems to be carrying on a conversation with himself and supplies his own response with what he wants the answer to be. If he does actually ask me a question, he persists and says it again.

I ask him, "Otto, why do you keep asking the same question?"

He retorts, "Because you don't give me the right answers!"

With our kids slowly becoming bilingual, Katy's Italian has also improved significantly. She doesn't speak it much, but she speaks flawlessly when she's upset. When she switches to Italian, the kids actually pay attention. They do, however, debate her points. I can't help but be proud to watch the boys argue in Italian and even use the appropriate hand gestures, no matter how creative.

## CORRECT ME IF I'M NOT WRONG

The daunting responsibility of raising kids weighs on us. Katy attends an open panel on bilingualism at the University of Minnesota that says if we don't start early, kids will never get the right accent. This confirms what we're doing, but I fear they'll just have my Minnesotan accent in Italian.

We figure that our kids can learn any language they want. Eilif went to German kindergarten and loved speaking *Deutsch*, but the teacher preferred the little girls who sat calmly in their seats and raised their hands. Eilif was too occupied sneaking his Superman costume into school under his Clark Kent outfit.

When the boys move on to elementary school, Eilif and Otto attend a Minneapolis Public School where a visiting instructor from Egypt teaches Arabic. The teacher is practically left mute by the frigid Minnesota winter. I ask the kids what they're learning, and they sing a song that turns out to be the Somali national anthem that their classmates taught them. "You know the American national anthem too, right?" I ask them.

They're not sure, so I sing a few bars. They've never heard it. Do we need to have American lessons too?

We sign up Eilif and Otto for Spanish lessons as my university job has dangled the possibility of a Costa Rica semester with a group of students. Katy likes the idea of escaping a Minnesota winter for the jungle and tropical beaches. Otto has decided Spanish is the same as Italian as long as you add an "s" to the end of each word.

Friends and relatives seem relieved that we're also learning a more "useful" language than Italian. I meet a man wearing a Masons pin who advises me that Spanish is indeed the most practical language. "I always studied Spanish because you never know when you're going to need to head south of the border to get away."

I look him over: a respectable man in his late fifties with a nice suit and bowtie. What is he up to that he needs to escape in a hurry?

"Did you know that Brazil has no extradition treaties?" he continues. "That's the best place to go, but then I found out that they speak Portuguese there . . ."

We meet a family who just moved back from three years in Costa Rica. They wouldn't tell us exactly what they did apart from "import–export." What the cargo was, we could only guess. They did divulge that Costa Rican public schools only meet for a few hours in the morning. Their kids added enthusiastically, "Then we were free for the rest of the day!"

We ask our boys' Spanish teacher if she's been to Costa Rica. She replies that in San José, Costa Rica's capital, they had to barricade their hotel door out of fear of being attacked. Perhaps we are fortunate that the Costa Rican opportunity falls through. The university promises that I'm first on the list for the next teaching opportunity abroad.

—

To bolster Eilif's waning interest in other languages, I tell him that he can become a spy when he grows up. He gets an old fedora from his cousins and insists on wearing it to a birthday party even though I tell him that there won't be spies there.

"Papà," he scoffs, "there are spies everywhere!"

Summer language learning is more successful. He and Otto stay at language camps where they speak German and Norwegian, but Eilif insists on learning Japanese now too. Apparently, everything cool comes from Japan: ninjas, origami, manga, sushi, samurai, and, of course, Pokémon. Otto prefers Spanish camp with its tacos and salsa dancing. Astri wants whatever Otto wants.

I love to hear the boys use new expressions in any language, but I get paranoid when Otto says, "Correct me if I'm not wrong. No wait. Correct me if I'm right."

Otto is often embarrassed of me when I speak to him in Italian in front of his friends. Perhaps he doesn't want attention drawn to his bilingualism. When I wonder if this bilingual experiment is a mistake, another parent compliments us for doing the "O.P.O.L." approach. She explains that this is "one person, one language" and considered a successful way to teach children a foreign language. I nod confidently, as if I have any clue what we are doing.

I find solace in articles that say bilingualism "protects the brain" and is "better than crosswords." The BBC reports that knowing two languages can "delay the onset of dementia by several years." I notice that our boys pick up other languages much more easily than I do, but they also forget words more quickly too. Even so, every parent I know who has bilingual children tells me that their kids sometimes waited until they were four or even five to speak. At that point, they could communicate in both languages.

One of Astri's first words is "*io!*" or "me!" in Italian because she saw her brothers blurting that out when they wanted something and she didn't want to miss out. She seems to understand everything. When we ask Astri if she wants something, her response sounds deceptively like "yeah–no" and "no–yeah."

Just when I'm wondering if I should switch back to English with her, my boss at work asks if I'd be interested in bringing students to Florence, Italy, for a few months. I think he felt bad that the Costa Rica trip fell through, so the school will at least pay for me to travel. The catch is that we must make our own arrangements if the whole family goes along. I see why most people don't travel far with kids: It's twice the adventure and cost. We'll be living in a tiny apartment in a brick city without a tree in sight.

I ask my family if they want to go. Astri replies "eee." I don't understand, so she nods her head. Otto translates helpfully that she's saying "yes" as "*Sììì!*"

WHILE I'M WORRIED that our kids will never learn Italian correctly, Katy is preoccupied with their being good people and not ending up behind bars. Her immediate concerns are that they'll hurt others or themselves. They'll eat too much or not enough. Instilling common sense seems impossible.

Eilif goes outside in shorts, a T-shirt, and sandals while snow is still on the ground. "It's sunny, so I'll be fine," he promises, only to run back inside.

Otto follows him outside on his scooter in a T-shirt. "Otto! You need a jacket," I warn him. "You might catch a cold!"

"That's not necessary," he assures me. "I already have a cold."

We worry that Otto often seems a bit distant and not socially engaged. He delayed talking when he was a baby, but his first words were a full phrase: "Thank you, Papà." We call him our "Buddha boy," since he observes rather than engages. We theorize that his detachment is a reaction to the chaos around the house. I'm concerned that my whole bilingual experiment is stunting his learning. When he does interact, he's often remote. "Life is like a quartz watch," he tells Katy dreamily.

"What the hell am I supposed to do with that?" she asks me.

He asks seemingly random questions: "What does God eat?" and "How do you give CPR to a giraffe?"

I tell him we need to work on small talk, like starting with the weather or asking how someone is doing. He has no time for that. Instead, he asks, "What do blind people see? Just nothing?"

His Italian is flawless, and he corrects me when I confuse masculine and feminine nouns, but then he blurts out, "Why doesn't anyone like Jimmy Carter? Wasn't he practically a saint?"

I respond, "Hmm, I suppose no one really likes saints because then they feel inferior around them."

Katy tries to dress him nicely so he doesn't look like a little ragamuffin, but Otto likes to wear the same T-shirt and shorts. She suggests a nice plaid shirt. "That's got buttons!" he protests. "Anything with buttons is formal!"

Otto ignores our advice and asks Google how often he should change his underwear because "you never tell me!"

He reads history books at a young age. Out of the blue, he wonders, "Why do they call it the Holy Roman Empire when it wasn't really an empire, wasn't Roman, and definitely wasn't holy." I don't know, but perhaps he doesn't expect a good answer from plebeians like us.

He declares disturbingly, "I'm going to be a Roman emperor someday."

"Umm . . . Great. Can we stay in your palace?" I ask.

He looks us over critically. "Hmm . . . I don't know."

We're worried that Eilif is too focused. I continue to push the Italian books and videos, but Pokémon is taking over his life. Katy asks him, "How about you go one day without talking about Pokémon? I'm sure your friends would be happy. We want to hear about all the other great sides of you."

"What? One day without Pokémon? What would I talk about?" he wonders.

He tells my brother Michael there are 721 Pokémon characters so far. Michael asks, "Really? Do you know them all?"

"Yeah!" Eilif begins to name them all with their special powers and how they evolve.

Michael stops him: "I believe you! I believe you!"

Eilif begs me to take him to a Pokémon convention in Boston. I tell him perhaps when he's older we can go to visit Boston's historical sites. "Who cares about that?" he replies. He sits down to write a letter to his older self that says, "Stay focused! Stay on target! Remember you must fulfill your mission to become a Pokémon Master!"

We can't help but diagnose our kids. Why does Astri draw a house and the roof isn't attached? Is this semi-abstract art like Picasso? She writes a story with the few words she knows—some in Italian, some in English. Instead of beginning in the upper left corner, she begins in the middle of the page and jumps all over the page like a word cloud. Why should we stifle her creativity to do it the "right" way?

ASTRI STRUGGLES with the two languages and wants me to read her books in English. To show her that it's better if we stick to Italian books, I read English with a ridiculous Italian accent. She loves it and demands, "More funny!"

I translate her English books into Italian on the fly, but I have to be careful that I'm using actual Italian words and not what I assume to be correct. I have a list of words for which the kids want a better translation, so I call my friend Giovanni in Milan.

"*Come si dice 'bulldozer' in italiano?*" I ask. How do you say "bulldozer" in Italian?

He just adds an Italian accent: "Bulldozer."

What about "puzzle"?

"Puzzle," he says, and explains that increasingly Italian is just becoming English.

This confuses Astri more than ever. If she doesn't know the word in Italian, she'll just say the English word with an Italian accent. Then she asks, "Papà, am I balingo?"

"Bilingual?" I ask. "*Sì.*"

"Is it cool to be balingo?"

Yes.

"Oh, then I'm definitely balingo!"

# LITTLE LEONARDO

Florence is arguably the most important city in the world for art, and we will live there. I show our kids books of the paintings of Michelangelo, Raphael, Botticelli, and Artemisia Gentileschi. I purchase several books on Leonardo da Vinci's experiments and Enzo Ferrari's handmade race cars, wishfully thinking that the kids will want to learn about these Italian inventors since we'll travel to Florence and Modena. Eilif casts the books aside, refusing to even open them. "Reading will be totally obsolete in fifty years," he declares.

I laugh. Eilif finally concedes, "Well, maybe we'll still be reading text messages in the future."

Just as I'm preparing to bring university students over to Italy for three months, 85-mile-per-hour winds sweep through our neighborhood in Minneapolis and knock down hundreds of trees. I worry we won't be able to go after all.

The storm leaves almost six hundred thousand homes without power. Eilif and Otto are thrilled by our current adventure of living by candlelight and eating all the ice cream from the freezer before it spoils. We journey outside on a sunny day after the storm to assess the damage to the neighborhood. The thwacking echo of axes ping-pongs through the air and chainsaws buzz to clear the debris. We climb over a giant elm that ripped up the sidewalk before falling across the street on a house. Eilif grins ecstatically at the damage and stutters, "It's, it's, it's . . . almost beautiful. It *is* beautiful." I explain that, yes, this sight is impressive and even awesome. It's not so beautiful for the people inside.

Perhaps the disaster triggers something in Eilif that inspires his benevolent side. Not only does he chip in to clean up all the branches in our neighborhood, but he takes Katy's complaints to heart that the kids aren't pulling their weight. Rather than simply putting his toys away as she has asked, Eilif conceives of a robot to deliver items to all rooms of the house. Perhaps inspired by the Leonardo book, he envisions an elaborate system of ropes connected to every corner of the house that his robot will zip around on, attached by a hook. Using his stash of tape, Eilif strings up ropes two to three feet from the ground throughout the house, stopping only when we point out that these are essentially trip wires. When Astri gets tangled in the string, he raises it just over her head so it nabs us in the neck. His dangling robot (essentially a cardboard box taped on a clothes hanger named Robox) bonks us on the head. He insists it's better to be hit on the head than trip on the rope.

To make matters worse, Eilif develops a slide down the steps from old grocery bags for the robot to glide on. Fortunately, he keeps the slide on only one side of the staircase so Astri doesn't tumble down into the basement.

"Eilif!" Katy shouts when she discovers all the materials he has used. "Next time you want to use your clothes for one of your projects, can you please tell me beforehand?" Eilif is adamant it was necessary to cut up his good corduroys to pin up on the corner of the wall. The robot couldn't make the turn down the steps without them. "I thought you wanted me to make your life easier!" he snaps. Katy curses me for introducing him to Leonardo's inventions because now Eilif thinks he can invent his way out of doing any work.

When Eilif's "delivery bot" doesn't run smoothly, he puts his effort into a "samurai robot" to fend off burglars. He takes his old red wagon, wraps tape around a cardboard box to secure a Japanese peasant hat on its head, and adds a plastic samurai sword to its front. "I call my robot *Cyber-i.* Get it? It rhymes with *samurai,*" Eilif announces proudly. He demonstrates how we only need to push it toward any intruder to impale them with the plastic sword and save our house.

Eilif discovers he needs propulsion for his machines. He concocts plans for a car that uses springs to move. This will "save everyone millions on gas. I can't believe that no one has thought of this before!" When neither Katy nor I can grasp his basic design, he laments that we just don't understand "how simple this is." He opts to build his invention alone and requires the proper tools: mostly tape, cardboard, and a stapler. "I need an axle and wheels," he explains, eyeing our car in the driveway. "This will be a toy car but will be as big as a real one and can carry people."

"How is that different from a real car?" I ask.

He shrugs off my small-mindedness and demands I supply him with an air conditioner. "Who wants to drive around in a hot car?" he asks. I burst his bubble by reminding him that an air conditioner weighs about fifty pounds. Undeterred, he requests a fan that will push the wheels. I show him that a fan would have a hard time blowing a gear unless it is a windmill. Instead, I suggest he harness the wind by raising a sail. He agrees: "Aha! I'll have the fan blow the sail!" I point out the limitations of having a long electrical cord to power the fan. I am the spoilsport who must point out potential flaws before he has a meltdown when his inventions fail to propel us into outer space.

Fortunately, his elementary school offers a program for budding inventors to create the next generation of automatons through Lego robotics. Eilif's rowdy peers frustrate him with their limited vision of how his inventions will transport us to a brave new world. I bring Astri to the final showcase of the Lego robotics of kids from all over Minneapolis. The announcer presents an award to Eilif's group. In fact, the teacher gives an award to every group since "We're all winners!" A jaded Astri mocks, "Blah, blah, blah . . ." in response.

Astri watches intently as Eilif creates new contraptions. Inspired, she embraces Scotch tape as an artistic medium to add to her scribbles. Astri grabs any tool she sees me use and walks around the house with an Allen wrench or screwdriver. She loosens any screw she can find, so our furniture wobbles precariously.

Astri always wants to button her own clothes and zip up her own jacket too. One Sunday in church she discovers Katy's new zip-up dress and unzips the back halfway down before Katy knows what is happening.

Astri adds glitter to her toolbox and soon it's everywhere: in pens, Christmas cards, nail polish, cookie decorations, and even bath bombs. It's in the air and my skin sparkles. Even the dog's poop in the backyard shimmers with glitter.

I ban glitter in the house as it can't be good to ingest. Astri is upset by this prohibition, but Eilif calms her with a giant cardboard box that all three of them fit in as a pretend Ferrari.

Eilif has finally cracked the book on Enzo Ferrari and drools over a photograph of a Testarossa. I tell him how expensive they are. "OK, I'll build one then!" he replies.

Otto points out that if he theoretically builds an identical car with all the parts, it won't be a real Ferrari.

Eilif announces he wants a Ferrari so bad that he'll save all of his money until he can get one. "I won't even rent an apartment or buy a house."

"Are you planning on living in our basement or in a cardboard box under the Lake Street bridge?" Katy asks.

"Why would I do that?" Eilif retorts. "I'm going to live in my Ferrari under the Lake Street bridge!"

Otto interrupts, saying his elementary school teacher drives a Lamborghini.

"No way, Otto. Do you know how expensive they are?" Eilif argues.

Otto insists it's a Lamborghini.

"Mom!" Eilif shouts. "Aren't Lamborghinis like half a million dollars?"

Otto won't back down, so Eilif slugs him.

## LEARN TO TWIRL SPAGHETTI LIKE A PRO

To prepare the kids to live in Tuscany, I tell them that Italy has the best food in the world, so we will spend a lot of time at the table. I work on their culinary skills and manners. I teach them how to boil pasta and properly swirl spaghetti around the tines of a fork. I demonstrate basic etiquette like using a fork with the left hand and a knife with the right. The kids think I'm being cruel.

To encourage our children to study Italian, we bribe them with snacks. Then they don't eat at meals. We make the snacks healthier and slowly reduce how many we give, but they demand more if they study. When we enroll them in any activity, inevitably the organizers pass around a sign-up sheet to bring snacks. The parents try to outdo each other with the most indulgent snacks.

I try to make the meals more appealing than the snacks. The kids do like to eat steak, but then I wonder why we are encouraging them to eat meat when we know raising animals for slaughter is inhumane. Is our excuse to raise our kids as carnivores just because meat tastes good and we need the protein?

At dinner, I mention an article I read about pigs being raised to be organ donors. Astri is outraged that they'd kill a pig to use its heart.

Otto points out, "Well, you eat bacon and sausages, so you're eating them anyway."

Astri protests, "I can eat a pig and still respect it!"

We cut down on meat and try to have snacks like fruit and nuts. Astri is skeptical, so she takes a bite out of each apple to see which one is the best. She takes the nuts, licks all the salt off each one, and puts them back. When Eilif discovers the bowl of nuts and trail mix that Astri left, he sits down and eats them as fast as he can chew.

I realize that as long as we're in the United States, it will be difficult to teach our kids how to eat healthy food as they do in Italy. Otto tells me that he saw a man on the Lake Street bus drinking a carton of heavy cream. "The guy got off the bus and then lit a cigarette. He'd alternate smoking and drinking whipping cream"—perhaps to see if he'd die first from lung cancer or heart failure.

Temptation is everywhere. When I hope that our kids will someday grow out of their gluttony for processed, sugary foods, I notice the diet of the college students I teach. While I'm getting ready for our upcoming stay in Italy, one of the students confesses that she doesn't eat well and is such a bad cook that her parents don't let her in the kitchen anymore. She tried to make popcorn by opening a can of creamed corn and putting it in the microwave. "It sparked and set off the fire alarm."

Another student complained about the high cost of the college cafeteria, so he bought a deluxe deep-fat fryer for his dorm room. "Grilled cheese sandwiches are *so* much better deep fried!" Each week he'd deep-fry something new: candy bars, Oreos, pickles, Twinkies. Over the course of the semester, I notice his complexion deteriorate and his whole body become a bit puffy. Even if his movements slowed down, he was happier than ever.

To introduce my students to Italian food, I go beyond gelato and Ferrero Rocher chocolate that everyone likes. I have them do a cheese tasting. Clio, a Chinese student, has never eaten cheese before and asks what is in it. I explain that cheese is aged, coagulated milk with mold. "Oh yuck!" She spits it out.

Some take my lessons on Italian food very seriously. A student is outraged by an Olive Garden advertisement for chicken Alfredo with unlimited breadsticks. "You lie!" she yells at the television. "That's not Italian food!"

I push them further with bitter chinotto soda, chunks of parmigiano, prosciutto crudo, and focaccia with black olives. The students describe the food as "challenging" since it isn't sugary. They cautiously poke at the food and explain that they've already had dinner before class. One student, Ayden, is clearly disappointed, "No spaghetti and meatballs? No pepperoni pizza? No Alfredo sauce? What's the point of learning Italian?"

I bring the leftovers home, and the kids eat everything since we're out of other sweet snacks. Perhaps it is true that if kids are hungry enough, they'll eat anything.

I think back to how my parents raised my brothers and me when we lived in Belgium. I remember my dad had European business friends over for dinner and he smoked cigarettes with them in the living room—something I'd never seen him do before. I begged to try one, so he gave me a puff. I was four. I coughed and wheezed and never wanted one again. I try this tactic on our boys when they beg us to try wine. Katy pours them each a mini glass of white wine. Eilif is thrilled and turns to his little brother: “Hey Otto! Let’s chug it! One, two, three—” Before we can stop them, they’ve downed their shots of wine. “Woo-hoo!” Eilif shouts and raises a fist.

Following this parenting failure, Katy assures me they’ll be fine. In fact, they’re ready for Italy.

CORTINA
TRENTO
VERONA
PROSECCO
PORCINI
GARDA
BRESCIA
POLENTA
MILANO
LAMBRETTA
ASTI
TORINO
GENOVA
SAN REMO
PALMANOVA
GALILEO!
PADOVA
VENEZIA
TRIESTE
PARMA
REGGIO
MARANELLO
MODENA
PROSCIUTTO
ACETO
BOLOGNA
RAVENNA
IMOLA
RIMINI
PISA
FIRENZE
LEGHORN
PONTEDERA
SAN MARINO
SIENA
ELBA
URBINO
ANCONA
ASSISI
COSTA SMERALDA
PESCARA
VATICANO
ROMA
SARDEGNA
CAGLIARI
CAFFÈ
NAPOLI
LA PIZZA
GELATO
FOGGIA
ISCHIA
VESUVIO
CAPRI
AMALFI
BUFALA
CALCIO
CAMPIONI DEL MONDO!
PAESTUM
BARI
TRULLI
ITALY
BRINDISI
STROMBOLI
CALABRIA
PALERMO
MARSALA
SICILIA
ETNA
CATANIA
AGRIGENTO

# PART II

# Florence at Last

## A MIRACULOUS ESCAPE FROM WINTER

"What? You and Katy are bringing your three kids to Italy for three months? Are you nuts?" That's the general reaction to our plan from friends who have traveled with children. The other is that "Eric will be gallivanting around Italy" and "eating at fancy restaurants"—obviously, those people don't have kids.

Katy and I jumped at the chance to live in Florence when my university confirmed that I can teach there for three months. We recognize it's financial folly to bring the whole family, as we still must pay for everyone's plane tickets and our house back in Minnesota as well as a place in Italy. The kids only have a vague idea of what this "Italy" is, despite their exposure to all things Italian.

Escaping a grueling Minnesota winter is incentive enough, but we'll be in Tuscany long enough to experience true day-to-day difficulties. If we must be around our wild, screaming children, can't we at least be around beautiful art? No other city (except maybe Rome) can come close to the sheer volume of art as Florence. Italian journalist Beppe Severgnini noted that just the basement storage of the Uffizi would be enough for major art shows in New York City for five years.

Art is the lifeblood of Florence. In 2007, art protestors filled the streets in front of the Uffizi because a Leonardo painting was to be sent to Japan. Florentine protesters chained themselves to the gate of the Uffizi to try and stop it. Then in 2017 Italian Culture Ministry Undersecretary Lucia Borgonzoni complained bitterly when the Uffizi agreed to lend Leonardo's *Annunciation* to the Louvre in Paris. "It's unfair, a mistaken deal. The French can't have everything they want," she told the newspaper *Corriere della Sera*. Disgusted that the Mona Lisa is at the Louvre in Paris rather than in Italy, she added, "In France, all he did was die."

The mayor of Florence, Matteo Renzi, declared that investment in art will save Italy and Europe. Most politicians think he's delusional, but they haven't calculated the return on investment that the Medici made centuries ago in Leonardo, Michelangelo, Raphael, Donatello, and others. Millions of tourists flock each year to Florence for the art. For us, will our stay in Florence be a good return on the investment? How can we even gauge that?

We begin preparations nearly a year in advance. A Swedish journalist offers to stay at our house for the three months, but Eilif and Otto think this is a terrible idea. "I don't want him messing with my stuff," Eilif threatens. I assure them that he really won't be interested in his Pokémon cards and stuffed animals.

"What if he moves my bed around or breaks my toys?" Eilif frets.

"Yeah, if anyone breaks my clay owl, I'll beat them up!" Otto exclaims.

"I'm going to sue them!" says Eilif. "Can we sue them, Papà?"

Otto proceeds to accidentally knock his owl off the shelf in his outburst. I have to fix it with superglue.

Katy wants to bring Bacco to Italy as well. After all, our dog is named for Bacchus, the god of wine. She does know it's impractical to fight the bureaucracy to register him for a European Union pet passport for just three months and even risk his being quarantined for the entire time we're in Italy. Instead, a family friend who dresses as Santa Claus every year for the kids offers to take him. Bacco isn't so convinced and barks viciously at this weird man in his obviously fake Father Christmas getup. Fortunately, the family of little Grace from across the street offers to take him on as a guard dog because their house has been burglarized twice. However, this then leaves our house unprotected.

Not only do we get the kids passports, but we make an appointment to make sure they're updated on their vaccines. Even though Eilif is the oldest child, he's horrified. The nurse pulls out a needle and Eilif makes a break for it. He runs down the hospital hall and hides in another room behind the table. We track him down, and both Katy and I have to hold him as he emits a blood-curdling shriek. When the nurse is done, he admits, "Oh, that wasn't so bad."

Katy asks Otto to please not make a scene because if he doesn't get the shot, he can't go to school in Italy. "Really? I don't have to go to school if I don't get the shot?" Before he can fully process this win–win situation, the nurse injects the medicine. He's only slightly annoyed by the needle. Astri is the bravest of all at two and a half years old. She barely even notices her shot.

Now, only two weeks before leaving, we are frantically preparing, but everything is going wrong. A February blizzard leaves us homebound; a mouse or two sneak into our house for warmth and gnaw into plastic bags in the pantry. The vacuum breaks, the scale to weigh our bags breaks, the refrigerator breaks—then our baby breaks.

Little Astri has trouble breathing due to the flu. I bring her to Urgent Care. The doctor immediately calls an ambulance to transport her to the hospital emergency room. I nervously accompany her in the ambulance with the EMTs in the back as they give her oxygen.

I call Katy, who rushes from home leaving a cryptic message with my family to come over to take care of the boys. My brother Michael comes to our house not sure of what has happened. He rings the doorbell and knocks. No answer. "Is anyone here?" he asks when entering. No one responds. He ventures into the basement where Eilif and Otto are busy playing video games now that their parents are away. "Hi guys! How's it going?"

"Great! We're playing Poképark on the Wii!" Eilif responds.

"Umm, where are your parents?"

"Oh, that's right," Eilif remembers. "They had to take Astri to the hospital!"

I KEEP MY COOL until the doctor hooks Astri up to a breathing tube. "You look like you need to sit down," a nurse says as my knees grow wobbly. I worry Astri might not make it. I glance at our precious two-year-old, who is unconscious and glassy.

As I sit outside the room, Katy pushes for answers. "We can't lose her, do you understand?" she demands.

The doctor informs Katy that Astri has serious pneumonia complicated by a staph infection, but she will probably survive. Our travel plans are long forgotten as we wait for days by her bed in the intensive care unit hoping for a recovery.

At the end of a week in the hospital, Katy and I prepare to cancel our flight the following week. The doctor remarks, "I don't see any reason why she can't fly in a few days."

"But she nearly died," Katy replies.

"Yes, but these little ones heal quickly." In fact, Astri is running around in a couple days after her return, blissfully oblivious to our trauma.

After that shock, I don't remember the dozens of details required to prepare a family of five to fly to Europe. Somehow, because of Katy's organizational skill, we manage to make it to the airport with our mounds of luggage. Without applying for an official visa, regulations allow us to stay in Europe for ninety days. I dutifully booked the airline tickets from March 1 to June 1.

As we're waiting in line to check in at the airport, I calculate that we'll actually be in Italy for ninety-one full days. If customs counts the travel days, we'll be there a total of ninety-three days. Katy is not pleased with my inability to count.

While waiting to board the flight, our family name is called over the intercom to approach the check-in desk. The airline service agent also noticed the discrepancy and asks me if we have a visa. I mumble a cryptic, unpersuasive answer that we won't need one. She remains unconvinced. For once in my life, I'm relieved that the boys start wrestling and Astri screams. Miraculously, instead of causing trouble for us, the stewardess allows us to board early to quiet down the kids. "You'll just have to work this out when you land in Italy," she warns.

Our flight touches down in Paris. We gather our carry-ons and struggle through the airport to find our connecting flight to Florence. I try not to act nervous about the possibility of the French customs agents not approving our extended stay. The windows with the guards ready to stamp our passports are at the far end of a maze of ropes intended for a long line, but we are the only ones here.

Rather than letting us skip right to the front, the amused French bureaucrats cruelly watch us navigate this labyrinth of metal poles and three-inch ribbons. We push and pull our five rolling carry-ons and five small backpacks. I hold Astri in one hand and with the other push a baby stroller stacked with bags and a child's car seat perched precariously on top. As we reach the end, a man behind the glass at passport control doesn't set down his cell phone long enough to greet us. He never looks us in the eyes as he wearily stamps our passports. We officially enter Europe.

I've been preparing the boys for our brief stopover in the Paris airport by teaching them short French phrases. I've tried to bribe them with bonbons to make the language attractive. Now here we are in France with two hours before our connecting flight. I ask them if they'd like some *chocolat chaud* and a *croissant.*

In French, I ask the waiter behind the counter for these treats. My French isn't good but is understandable. In response, the waiter rolls his eyes, repeats my order in an exaggerated American accent to mock me, and laughs. Oh, kids, I forgot to tell you that the French can also be rude bastards. Perhaps in solidarity, the kids don't even like their hot chocolate.

FIRENZE
TUSCAN SUN
BEATRICE
BOLOGNA
MODENA
PRATO
SAN MARINO
VENEZIA
RIMINI
SANTA MARIA DEL FIORE
BAPTISTERY
COLLODI
FORTEZZA DA BASSO
SCOPPIO DEL CARRO
BONFIRE OF THE VANITIES
BARGELLO
SANTA CROCE
CALCIO FIORENTINO
SANTA MARIA NOVELLA
STROZZI
FERRAGAMO
UFFIZI
ZECCA THE MINT
BISTECCA
PORCELLINO
ARNO
MICHELANGELO
MUD ANGELS
SANTO SPIRITO
SCHIACCIATA
CHIANTI
BOBOLI
LA PESTE
ABANDON ALL HOPE
FONDATA 59 BCE
I. LIMBO
II Lust
III. GLUTTONY
IV. Greed
V. ANGER!!
VII. VIOLENCE
IX. TREACHERY
THE DREGS
TRAMONTANA
GRECALE
LEVANTE
SCIROCCO
OSTRO
LIBECCO
PONENTE
MAESTRALE

## PIE BRIBES

We shed our winter coats and descend onto the tarmac holding our kids' hands to avoid an accidental cartwheel onto Italian asphalt. Katy asks the smartly dressed Italian airline employee where our checked bags might be.

"How should I know? Go check the lost and found!"

Katy responds, amazed: "Really? You don't know where our bags go?"

"Welcome to Italy!" he tells her and points to the waiting bus that is already full with other passengers from our flight. "Get on right away!" he orders us.

I look at our mound of carry-on luggage and our two-year-old who insists on being carried. I suggest we wait for the next one.

"There won't be another bus. You must squeeze inside," the man demands. "Some of the children can go in different doors."

"You want us to separate from our children?" Katy asks in disbelief. Astri screams and the sympathetic passengers help us scrunch inside.

The driver accelerates around the curves painted on the

tarmac. We're pushed violently left and right but are so squeezed together that no one falls down. The brakes squeal and the bus stops after a mere two hundred yards. "It would have been easier to walk!" Katy quips.

Our suitcases arrive down the conveyor belt intact. No one is at customs to inspect what contraband we might be smuggling in. No one checks our passports to see if we'll be staying beyond our ninety-day limit.

OUR APARTMENT is wedged between the Arno River and the church of Santo Spirito in a piazza full of antique vendors and artist cafés. We're perched on the third floor of a fourteenth-century *palazzo* (palace) with no elevator. We convince ourselves that this will help us get in shape. The spotless marble flights of stairs are less attractive when we have to haul up our fifteen suitcases.

The tall, arched ceilings make us forget that five of us will be squeezed into a two-bedroom apartment for the next three months. The terra-cotta tiles underfoot are loose and the floor shakes slightly when we walk. The walls tremble when the boys tramp through. Katy remarks that this is a cement building and shouldn't creak like our 1920s wooden home back in Minnesota.

Our landlady, Fede, warns us that the people in the apartment below took out a wall. "But we had the engineers come and they said that it shouldn't affect the structure of the building," she promises. "Still, we shouldn't put lots of books or heavy objects in that room and please don't move the furniture."

"So the boys shouldn't run or jump in that room, right?" I ask.

Fede, who doesn't have kids, looks to see if I'm joking. I'm not. "Oh no, there are neighbors on all sides. They must be quiet."

Keeping the kids silent proves the most difficult aspect of our time in Florence. The artists and students out on the street, however, bang around all night below. Fede claims she installed expensive noise-reducing windows, but they only have one pane of glass and no screens or storm windows. Katy is constantly woken by scooters, horns, singing, and merry-making at all hours that echo up the walls to our windows.

At a quarter to eight in the morning, the street is already jammed with students in brightly colored backpacks and deliverymen hauling in artichokes and wild boar to the *ristoranti.* Scooters impatiently weave around elderly women leisurely crossing against red lights. "When do these Italians sleep?" Katy wonders. We see a very serious looking businesswoman in a corduroy power suit. Her T-shirt underneath is in English script with glitter: *Party all night; sleep all day.*

Fede is pleased—and seems almost surprised—that we pay our rent on time. Perhaps interpreting this as us having more money than we do, she informs us that when Katy's parents come to visit for a few days, we need to pay an extra 150 euros "because the water is so expensive."

She asks if it's all right for her to report to the government that we only pay half as much. "Otherwise they'll tax me more and then you'll just have to pay more." Her scheme seems fine, I suppose. We agree, even if this wasn't the original agreement. Because we are willing to work with her, she leaves us a delicious fruit pie the following week.

## PREPARE TO ENVY YOUR CHILDREN

Our Italian friend Carlo warned us about signing the kids up for Italian public school: "You will spend all of your time navigating the bureaucracy, getting signatures, and signing documents. By the time you get them into school, it will be time to come home." Instead we opt for a private Italian art-based K–6 school called "Kindergarten," even though Eilif is insulted as he's in fourth grade. The principal informs us that it's best if the boys aren't graded since we'll only be here for three months.

The tuition for each boy is almost $700 a month, which we can scarcely afford. The school keeps adding extra expenses that hurt our pocketbook because of the terribly weak dollar. The Italian parents seem eager to cough up cash for fabulous field trips, while we can barely scrounge up enough euros for their school supplies. Most of the parents seem to have just one child, which might explain Italy's negative birth rate. The old stereotypical Italian family of many rugrats struggling to survive has been replaced by pampered princes and princesses dressed in the best Benetton or Stefanel outfits.

Our boys aren't convinced that Italian school is such a good idea. They are visibly nervous entering a foreign classroom, even if they can understand most of the Italian. The first day, both Eilif's and Otto's teachers open their doors and give the boys bear hugs and multiple kisses on the head. They melt with relief at the warm welcome. I soon deduce that perhaps all this hugging and kissing is why lice are so rampant at the school.

The boys are thrilled with the free spirit of the school—no one scolds them if they run in the hall, and everyone seems to like how "*vivace*" (lively) they are. They're fueled by frequent Nutella snacks and freshly made, three-course lunches of pizza Margherita, fresh mozzarella cheese balls, risotto, and *prosciutto cotto.* "They're eating far better than we are," Katy points out. Still, I can't resist living vicariously when the boys tell us what they had each day for their *primo* and *secondo* (first and second courses) while at school.

What's more, their classes take regular outings to local landmarks. Our kids already missed this year's trips to the Galileo Museum, the Uffizi, and the climb up the cathedral's dome. Eilif's class goes to the Da Vinci Museum in Florence to see models of Leonardo's inventions. This is followed by a trip to the town of Vinci to see where the Renaissance master's revolutionary ideas began. Eilif tells us that we never appreciated his own inventions at home, but maybe because we never gave him the proper materials. Despite these amazing field trips, Eilif laments, "At home, the teachers just tell us, 'Have fun!' But here in Italy, it's like 'You better learn this!'"

Otto's second-grade class settles on a daylong trip to the Mediterranean to the city of Livorno, strangely called "Leghorn" in English. Eilif, on the other hand, informs us that his entire fourth-grade class will travel to Turin to the Egyptian museum and then to the steep mountains of Val d'Aosta near

France for two nights. Who in their right mind would take a gaggle of forgetful, know-it-all ten-year-olds to a major city and then to precipitous cliffs?

"That's just what we do!" the principal tells me. Indeed, nearly all Italian classes beginning in about third grade take major trips around Italy.

Their classmates are well traveled. While I am proud that our kids speak two languages, I admit that this is the first time we've been able to bring them out of the country. Eilif's classmate from Norway speaks Italian, English, and Norwegian fluently. A twelve-year-old boy from Senegal manages French, Italian, and English, plus two Senegalese languages. Florence is such an international city that many of the children have lived abroad as well.

Still, Italian pride remains intense. Otto wears a T-shirt from the local department store that has "Brazil" silkscreened across the front because that country is hosting the World Cup. His classmates are upset and question his loyalty: "What's wrong with Italia?" Otto's frown is like an umbrella, however, and when it's turned over he wins back all the affection of his classmates.

Even if Otto risks alienating his new friends by not wearing the proper soccer jersey, Eilif complains that Otto is having a much easier time. Eilif usually makes friends immediately, but he reports that the fourth grade is tough: "Second graders aren't really Italian yet," and Otto is around those younger kids that aren't quite fully formed by their culture.

Many aspects of the school take some getting used to. Rather than fire drills, earthquake drills are the norm. One of the teachers tells me, "We're lucky that we don't need to do volcano drills, as they do in Sicily for Etna and Naples for Vesuvius."

The biggest nuisance proves to be much smaller. One day while combing the boys' hair, Katy leaps back, "They're moving! He has bugs in his hair!" In spite of our preventative herbal anti-lice spray, all the hugging and kissing helped spread these creatures around the school. I assure Katy that these are surely sophisticated Italian lice.

As though she knew this would happen, Katy brought two lice combs. We spend the next days pulling out little specks from their hair. For once in my life, I'm happy that I'm losing hair.

Katy reminds me of a little girl in Eilif's kindergarten class in Minnesota who had lice. The mother was embarrassed and frustrated trying to get rid of them. When the class gathered in a circle to talk about the problem, the teacher tried to keep it anonymous: "Someone in the class has a problem with lice so we—"

"That's me!" the girl interrupted excitedly. "Hey everyone, she's talking about me! I'm the one with lice!"

Otto's Italian teacher commiserates with us as the tiny insects have been passed repeatedly through the school. "Yes, the lice are a nightmare. If you find them, you have to wash everything."

We pull the kids from school for a few days to pass our time hauling our lice-infested laundry over the Ponte Vecchio and through the Piazza della Signoria to the laundromat. We spend more than fifty dollars on dryers alone. While waiting for the washing machines, we take a field trip to the Bargello National Museum next door. We see medieval suits of armor and clothes, and I take this as a "teachable moment" that nearly everyone in the Renaissance was teeming with lice and fleas. Katy shudders.

After our negative reaction to the bugs, Eilif says with delight, "I read in [the Italian comic] *Geronimo Stilton* that in old England, people were proud to have lice." Perhaps the boys don't regard our infestation as a disgusting battle but rather that we are reliving the Renaissance.

When the boys return to school, Otto's teacher gives us a sympathetic glance knowing what we've been through. Still, she keeps her distance from him for a while.

The week before Mother's Day, Otto proudly brings home a special gift for Katy that all the kids made for their mammas. Katy opens it proudly as Otto says it's "*la pagella per la mamma.*"

"What? A report card?" Katy asks, insulted but laughing. "You're grading me now?"

She opens up the slip that shows she only gets a four out of ten in creativity, but ten in driving, cooking, and cuddling. Otto awards her a perfect score in patience, which even she admits is delusional. Even though she's been a stay-at-home mom, she only gets a four for working around the house because she doesn't know how to fix doorknobs. The harshest score is a measly one in athletics. I remind her that the kids are just auditing their classes here in Italy, but apparently we're the ones who need to improve our grades.

## INVEST IN ART

Since we're staying three months in Florence, we invest a hundred euros in an *Amici degli Uffizi* (Friends of the Uffizi) card, which is valid for free entrance to all the Florentine state-run museums for a year. We skirt by the lengthy lines with the card—essential for little ones who won't wait an hour.

I ponder how to keep squirrelly boys from practicing their all-star wrestling moves among the pensive art lovers. It's almost amusing how boys tackling each other in front of Botticelli paintings unnerves museum guards. Katy wisely outfits the boys with little scavenger hunt books about the art we see, so they can earn their gelato. The treasure hunt booklets turn into a competition despite our best efforts that they should work together. Instead, they punch each other when the other gets more points.

Some themes of the art are decidedly un-family-friendly. (Try explaining Giambologna's sculpture *Rape of the Sabine Women*. Definitely adult material.) Still, the boys are fascinated by Giuliano de' Medici being assassinated in the cathedral and his brother Lorenzo narrowly escaping through a secret passage. They're intrigued by the tale of the priest Girolamo

Savonarola's "bonfire of the vanities," lit after convincing the Florentines to torch everything decadent: makeup, jewelry, books—even Botticelli burned his paintings—in the main square, Piazza della Signoria.

"That doesn't make any sense," Eilif says.

I tell them that Savonarola and other devout monks would beat themselves with a flail.

"Why would he do that?"

I explain that they wanted to be more like Jesus and suffer as he did when he was beaten by the Roman jailers. Savonarola then condemned the pope in Rome for his excesses and ended up burned at the stake himself.

Otto says, "I didn't know people could burn."

Eilif points to a painting. "And that naked guy on the cross, is that Jesus?"

Katy decides that Eilif needs more religious education since we see these symbols and paintings everywhere. Eilif isn't pleased when she pulls out a six-hour *Jesus of Nazareth* DVD. "Why all this Jesus stuff?" Eilif complains. He isn't satisfied with the answer that kids "just need to know this."

In the film, Joseph is confused that Mary is pregnant, and he swears he didn't touch her. Eilif says, "Sorry Joseph, God got to her first!"

"Eilif!" Katy says, shocked.

"I'm just sayin'," he replies.

The film obviously isn't having the desired effect. We tire of the movie after the first half hour.

To lure the boys back into the art, we climb. We ascend the cathedral and its bell tower. We go on the secret passage tour of the old city hall, Palazzo Vecchio. We discover trap doors, a hidden passage behind the map of Armenia to the Vasari

Corridor escape route that weaves more than a kilometer through a Renaissance skyway above the town.

The docent leads us into the dark attic, a maze of giant beams holding up the roof that is roped off to visitors. Eilif asks her, "Can I go up there? I'll bet it would hold me."

She responds, "That's why they close it off, so little boys don't fall through the ceiling."

Katy volunteers to stay with Astri while the boys insist I take them up the steep tower of the Palazzo Vecchio. I ask them to go slowly since I get vertigo. They can't resist skipping steps, jumping down four or five at a time, climbing to the edge and peering out dangerously hundreds of feet below. Fortunately, iron grates close off the scariest parts, including the trap doors that look down on the Hercules and David statues 150 feet below. Eilif decides to test the old metal by jumping up and down on top of it to see if it will break. I'm horrified and paralyzed, but the metal holds. He's somehow disappointed.

I prefer the safety of museums where I don't have to worry about falling children. I show them Donatello's nude of David, but they say he looks more like a girl, apparently because of his long hair and floppy hat. The boys are embarrassed by the "naked pictures," but Astri doesn't seem to notice. Titian's famous *Venus of Urbino* of a well-endowed woman lounging nude on a couch makes the boys cringe, but Astri shouts, "Doggie!" when noticing the curled-up little puppy on the sofa. The boys prefer Caravaggio's wide-eyed, decapitated Medusa head on a shield and Artemisia Gentileschi's Judith chopping off the head of Holofernes. Terrible, yes, but kind of cool, they say.

All this blood and gore makes them want to try this for themselves. Perhaps they've learned a bit too much from the

statues of Romulus and Remus because, like all good brothers, they soon grab sticks and duel. Fortunately, our *Amici degli Uffizi* card gives us unlimited entrance into the Boboli Gardens, but the signs everywhere warn, "*È vietato calpestare le aiuole*," it's prohibited to walk on the flower bed or essentially any grass. In other words, even the parks are pieces of art, so no dueling on the lawn.

## STOPLIGHTS ARE MERELY RECOMMENDATIONS

Some of the narrow medieval sidewalks are barely eighteen inches wide and cars zip past, so the protruding mirrors nearly clip our elbows. I'm terrified we'll lose one of the kids to a speeding motorist, but Eilif assures me on our second day, "Don't worry Papà, I have the Italian roads all figured out." Really? I've lived in Italy for four years and still don't understand.

Fortunately, signs in the historic center tell us that most streets are pedestrian only. That is, the only vehicles allowed are police cars, fire trucks, ambulances, *carabinieri*, *vigili di finanza* (treasury police), delivery trucks, taxis, local residents, and any scooter that can evade the traffic cops. One of the Florentine parents at the school tells me, "At least cars don't go on the sidewalks as they do in Naples."

I try to teach the boys to obey the lights at the intersection, but our Neapolitan friend Guido points out that "red stoplights are recommendations." He tells me that we Americans like things to be black and white, but nothing works that way in Italy. "Do you want to submit to authority?" It's a political

question. Even if the light is green, we're not necessarily safe to cross. In other words, our kids need to look out.

Katy and I are talking outside a pizzeria when two Aprilia scooters going the wrong way down a one-way street zip within inches of Astri's stroller. The owner of Trattoria Nerone shrugs it off, saying, "What can you do? We live in a republic. Sure, the police can take their licenses if they're caught, but in a democracy, they think they have a right to break the law."

Pedestrians have only won the battle in the main tourist spots, where even taxis give up trying to get through phalanxes of tourists. I'm worried that we'll simply lose the kids in a crowd. Our friend Anna from Milano says that she wrote her two boys' names and addresses on their arms in case they got separated. I just want our kids to acquaint themselves so well with the city center that they can always find their way home.

The boys look up to Giotto's bell tower when it tolls to keep themselves on time for school. Possessive little Astri points to the campanile and cathedral and tells her brothers, "Mine!" as if they were trying to keep it for themselves.

I tell them about architect Filippo Brunelleschi's incredible feat of finishing the cupola over the cathedral with Renaissance-era technology. Eilif looks up at the giant red roof: "Papà, were you alive when Brunelleschi built his dome?"

Katy originally planned to have the kids use kick scooters to get around town, but the sidewalks and streets prove far too unpredictable. We need someplace to take them to run around since they have to stay quiet in the apartment. We let them loose in the piazza in front of Santa Maria Novella where others gather to chat and enjoy the excitement. We set them free on their scooters on the bumpy flagstones to jump, swerve, and veer dangerously close to Italians on their leisurely Sunday strolls. None of the locals say a word to reprimand the boys and even chuckle at their joy. I realize that this is why I love Italy: No one even thinks of ruining your fun.

This extends to safety too. We bundle them up in helmets and cover their knees to avoid injuries on their scooters. As we watch the kids take over the piazza, Katy says, "I was wondering why all the little kids on their parents' bicycles are so cute here. Then I figured out that none of them have helmets." They ride on little seats attached to the handlebars or a crude one on the rack behind the seat. Some even stand on the rear rack of the bicycle and hold on to their parents' shoulders. Booster seats for kids in cars are apparently optional. Even the taxi driver from the airport was surprised when we had a car seat for Astri and simply had all five of us squeeze into his cab with no seatbelts for the joyride to our apartment in Santo Spirito.

In the old days, a journey to the dark side happened in our neighborhood of Santo Spirito. Michelangelo followed a papal decree that allowed him to dissect cadavers in the monastery in exchange for his work on a wooden crucifix for the church. Today, no artist is slicing up bodies, but the church steps have become a hangout for drunks. Otto asks me, "Why are those guys always here?" I tell him that this is what happens if you don't study at school.

Soon enough, the boys have to use the bathroom, but they don't want to go all the way to our apartment and up three flights of steps. I look around for a public restroom when I notice one of the day drinkers walk over to the side of the Santo Spirito church and unzip his pants. He realizes I'm shocked. He has the courtesy to move twenty feet farther away before peeing on the church. Without drawing attention to him, I scurry the kids on their scooters away and discourage Astri from splashing in puddles of mysterious liquid.

Despite the dirty sidewalks and squares, I'm always impressed by the absolute cleanliness of Italian clothes and apartments. I wonder if little has changed from the medieval days when chamber pots were dumped out the windows. Then I notice that the streets and squares of Florence are cleaned early almost every morning. Back in Minneapolis, the street-sweeping truck passes twice a year, but here special vehicles make sure even the sidewalks and walls are clean for tourists.

I tell the boys that they can't just pee on the church walls, and we have to shell out a euro for a public toilet. "Why should we have to pay to pee?" Eilif asks incredulously, perhaps remembering the documentary we saw on Pompeii that showed the Romans using urine to clean clothes. Plus Francesca, a friend from Florence, told us that blonde hair was the fashion during the Renaissance, so women used horse pee to dye their hair yellow.

Our urine isn't so valuable, so I teach them how Italian toilets work. Amidst lots of giggles, I show them that the brush is to clean the toilet after using it. I warn them: "Eilif, don't use the brush on your teeth, OK?" They laugh and then ask about the bidet. They find it hard to believe it's not a toilet but for cleaning oneself afterward. Astri wiggles her index finger emphatically, "No, no, no!" pointing at the bidet.

We would go broke with all of Astri's false alarms to use a restroom. Instead, Katy planned ahead by bringing a portable potty for toddlers that vacuum seals the waste inside. Astri decides that she can use her potty wherever she wants. It's much nicer to do her business outside with a spectacular view of the green rolling hills of Tuscany than in some dingy, urine-soaked hole. In the Uffizi Gallery, however, she can't open it up under a Leonardo painting, so a guard asks people admiring the art to make room for the little princess. He leads us through several side storage rooms to use the elevator for the stroller to get downstairs. We get a secret tour of brilliant paintings leaning against the wall that no one but the janitor sees.

Astri in her stroller is our secret weapon to part the waters for us in the piazzas as well. Bring a toddler to Florence to sneak through crowds. Sometimes, though, the sight of Astri draws people closer. A little old lady puts her hands to her cheeks, exclaiming "*Che meraviglia!*" (What a marvel!). Even slick young Italian men in the latest Armani fashions break their stride to take a look at the little star.

Astri is haughty, though, and far more interested in pointing out doggies and other Italian kids her age who still have pacifiers. When she sees the Virgin Mary or posters of Botticelli's red-haired beauty in *The Birth of Venus*, she exclaims, "Mamma!"

A group of Asian tourists with headphones and identical pink hats are distracted at the sight of our little cherub. Their guide, who is speaking into a microphone and holding up an antenna with a pink tassel, keeps walking, unaware that her group has stopped to adore Astri. Who needs the Palazzo Vecchio with the copy of Michelangelo's *David* when a real, live angel is here? Katy is a bit freaked out by all the attention to Astri: "It's bizarre! Sure, she's cute, but what the hell?"

The tourists take turns having their photo snapped with Astri, but she is not pleased. We push through the crowd. When the tourists finally move on, Astri notices the giant David statue. She points and declares, "Papà!" Good girl.

## BUDDING GLADIATORS

One day walking back from the boys' school, we nearly lose them amidst throngs of visitors following guides holding up flags for their groups in front of the old city hall, Palazzo della Signoria. We finally recover the boys and Otto complains, "I don't like all these tourists."

"But Otto, you're a tourist!" Eilif points out.

"Oh yeah . . ." he replies, remembering that he isn't Italian. I tell them we'll see even more tourists this weekend when we visit Rome.

Eilif notes that compared to Americans, people in Florence are "kind of the same. Kids like Pokémon just as much." His one complaint about Italy is "I just can't believe how expensive Pokémon cards are here!" Even so, he spends any euros he has on more trading cards.

To get his mind off his obsession with this Japanese game, I point out the marble statues, the Renaissance architecture, and the dark medieval alleys. Eilif, in all his preteen glory, merely shrugs. Then he lights up, "You know, though, this city reminds me a lot of the Poképark video game."

I suggest that perhaps this is because video games are based on real cities. Does art imitate life? Do video games recreate cities? "Oh, that could be . . ." he ponders, finally interested.

Ever since they were little, Eilif and Otto have been obsessed with advertising and how to use the products correctly. When their grandfather Bumpa took them to McDonald's back in Minneapolis to buy *Ice Age* Happy Meals, they discovered little figurines of two of the characters. The two tots then wanted to see the film related to these product tie-ins, so Katy let them watch it. The movie was rated PG, though, and Eilif and Otto were too scared to continue. Eilif told Otto, "At least we now know what we do with these guys: They fight!" They then mashed the action figures against each other in mortal combat.

I played plenty of Atari when I was little, but I can't help blaming the new video games when I see Eilif and Otto whack each other on the streets of Florence just for fun. I want to believe that they are little angels corrupted by the world around them, but I know better. Katy and I don't buy them toy weapons, but still Otto makes a pistol out of his cheese sandwich to make-believe he's blasting his brother.

Eilif is always surprised when Otto actually cries after he's punched. "Did you really just slug him?" Katy asks.

"No! I mean . . ." Eilif hesitates. "Well, I didn't hit him *that* hard!"

Even the classic game of tag becomes a game of "slug," a never-ending punching game. At the end of the school day in Florence, Eilif sneaks up on Otto and wallops him on the back. While Otto is wailing, I scold Eilif that he has to stop hitting his little brother.

"It's part of a game!" he screams, as if I'm an unfair referee.

"And you, Otto," Katy chimes in, "if you're going to play these games with Eilif, you have to stop complaining if he hits you back." Otto is upset that he didn't do anything, so he hits Eilif. The game continues.

The next day, Eilif hits Otto again right after school and I tell him to stop. "I have to hit him! It's the new rules that mamma made yesterday. I get to hit Otto whenever I want!"

Back in Minnesota, I tried to teach them about nonviolent heroes such as Gandhi, Martin Luther King, and the Quakers. "The who?" Eilif wanted to know, and I pointed out the drawing on the Quaker Oats cereal box of the smiling man with a white wig. Otto read on the box about a special contest to win $50,000 in honor of the company's fiftieth anniversary. Eilif excitedly opened the box, certain that he'd win. He was crushed when he pulled out a little note inside the box that said he didn't win but could save fifty cents on the next box of cereal. Katy consoled him, saying that no one ever seems to win those contests. She joked that the CEO of Quaker Oats probably won it as a bonus.

This gave Eilif an idea. "Hey Otto, if he won, we can go beat him up and take his money. He can't fight back since he's a Quaker!"

I tried a different tack, reminding them that superheroes are very strong but only use violence as a last resort. "They only use their powers for good and to stop the bad guys." Eilif studied these superheroes with their special skills and realized that indeed they don't pick fights but are ready to retaliate.

He told me he needed a "six pack." I confessed that I didn't know what this meant. Eilif described the six muscle rolls he wanted on his stomach. When I took him for his annual checkup, the doctor listened to his chest. Eilif tensed his stomach and proclaimed, "I just have a two pack now, but I almost have a four pack!"

Rather than doing all the sit-ups, weightlifting, and waiting until puberty hits, Eilif demonstrated his strength simply by donning his puffed-up Spider-Man costume equipped with foam muscles. He wore this around thinking that we'd be convinced he was suddenly buff. One perk he learned from wearing these puffy muscles was that he couldn't feel the pain when Otto whacked him. Now in Rome, Eilif realizes that the padding protects him from his brother poking him with his new plastic gladiator sword. Otto is frustrated that his sword isn't working on Eilif's stomach, so he just thumps Eilif over the head with it.

I imagine this violence will fade now that they have a sweet little sister. I warn the boys to be gentle with her because she wants to imitate their actions. Sometimes they do calm down and play with her stuffed white kittens. The three little kitties coo and meow, thanks to Eilif and Otto's sound effects, but the boys can't resist putting them into a cage match to see which would win in a fight to the death.

To get their minds off the stuffed animal brawl, we all watch *Ben-Hur* in our apartment, thinking that perhaps the studies are correct that we can get our aggressions out vicariously by video games and films. Astri watches the action for a few minutes and then notices that the boys have finally set down their toys. She picks up Eilif's gladiator sword and shouts, "Hiya!" as she whacks both Otto and Eilif on the head.

That's when I figure that if the kids want violence so much, at least they can learn about historical violence. We'll be in Rome for a few days, so I give them books about the gladiators and ancient Romans. Eilif is appalled that Julius Caesar plucked all the hair from his body every day. "Wouldn't that hurt?" Never mind that he was stabbed by forty senators.

When we step inside the Colosseum, I expect them to be thrilled to envision the mock naval battles, lions attacking humans, and gladiators fighting to the death just to please Caesar. Instead, they are bored even after the gladiator films we've seen. Perhaps they were expecting actual gladiators. Or maybe they caught on that I was using the idea of ancient slaughters to educate them about history. I give up.

Otto pipes up, "Hey Eilif, imagine if they had Pokémon battles in the Colosseum."

"Whoa! That would be so cool!" Eilif replies, finally interested. Perhaps the lessons worked after all as they envision their little stuffed Pokémon as ancient Roman gladiators.

# HOLY FIRE

Eilif and Otto are no longer afraid to run off down the streets or zoom around on their kick scooters. We are no longer just sightseers. Sixteen million visitors come to Florence annually and are required to pay a tourist tax of four to eight euros for each night. Tourists only have to pay for the first week, potentially filling the city coffers with hundreds of millions of euros a year. Our landlady Fede cryptically informs us, "You're different, so we don't need to pay this." We don't argue.

As we forget about our life back in the United States, we start to rely on services here. Astri is stricken with another cold, and I worry that we took her out of the hospital back home too soon. We stop in the drugstore for some cough syrup and the pharmacist gives me a homeopathic remedy without even asking if I prefer it to Western medicine. Outside the store, I look at the sign that says "*farmacia*," pharmacy, as well as "*erboristeria*," herbalist. They tell me that most people now use herbal cures before using modern medicine.

I complain that I have a sore elbow, probably tendonitis, from shoveling snow back in Minnesota. The herbalist sells me fifty euros worth of "Devil's Claw" gel capsules and a stinky spray that smells like a mix of myrrh and urine. "If this doesn't work, stop back and we can try some other herbs," she tells me after I pay. This doesn't build my confidence, but I am impressed by the stories on these ancient remedies from monks at remote monasteries. I wish I could say that her cure worked like a shot, but the aches continue and I smell like aromatic pee. I am hesitant to spring for more herbs at such steep prices. If we had residency in Italy, the government could send us to one of the health spas that are covered by the Italian public health care system. Perhaps we could even get a pass to the new store in Florence that has water tanks filled with Turkish minnows that chew the dead skin off one's feet. I don't see any tourists in that store.

WE FIGHT THE LINES in front of the Galleria dell'Accademia and manage to get in to see the pinnacle of Western art. I explain that Michelangelo's *David* is a symbol of the Renaissance, Florence, and the perfection of the human body. After the hardships of bringing a family across the ocean, I hope the boys will finally be inspired by this nearly flawless piece of art. Otto just points at the beautiful nude of David and giggles.

To get the boys interested in the local dialect, I point out to Otto that the Italian language comes from Florence because Dante wrote the *Inferno* not in Latin, but in Tuscan.

"Inferno, that means 'hell'!" he says, rather pleased that he can cuss. I explain that it's not a bad word in Italian, even if people from Tuscany are famous for swearing. I tell him that Dante had to leave the city to avoid being killed and ended up buried in Ravenna. Now Florence wants his bones back.

"Why would they want some dead guy?"

I explain that *La Divina Commedia* is the most important book in Italian and made Tuscan the language everyone in Italy uses, even if they have a funny accent. In Florence, the "k" sound isn't pronounced and is replaced with an "h" sound. "Instead of *casa*, they say *hasa*," I tell him. "Instead of Coca-Cola, they say Hoha-Hola."

Otto thinks a minute, "So rather than *cucchiaio* [spoon], they say 'huhiaio.'"

"Yes."

"Instead of *cacca*," or poop, "they say *haha*, right?"

"I suppose so," I reply, not happy about the turn of the conversation.

"I eat my *haha* with a *huhiaio*," he laughs. He is excited that he has a joke to tell his classmates.

Here in Florence, nearly everyone can speak English well because of all the tourists. Newspapers and television shows are peppered with English words because they apparently sound much more sophisticated, but the meaning is often skewed. We hear an announcement on the train in garbled English for a "welcome drink" with a "friendly snack." Rather than actually speaking Italian, Otto prefers to tie together these clumsy English phrases with an Italian accent and excessive hand gestures. He laughs as I wonder why I bothered teaching him Italian.

APART FROM THE ACCENT, the Florentines have other odd traditions. As if present-day soccer isn't violent enough, they have their own Renaissance version called "*calcio fiorentino*" that allows punching, choking, elbowing, and head butts, all just to get the damn ball in the goal. Modern spoilsports don't allow kicking to the head. I don't think I need to show the kids this Italian all-star wrestling football.

Instead, we file into the square in front of the cathedral at Easter for the "*Scoppio del Carro,*" or explosion of the cart. I tend to think of Easter in terms of flowers and newborn baby animals. Instead, Florentines sandwich into the square to blow things up. As the story goes, a member of the Pazzi family was the first to scale the walls of Jerusalem to attack the city during the First Crusade. (Oddly, a member of this family later stabbed to death one of the Medici brothers as he prayed in Florence's cathedral.) In reward for the Pazzi's bravery during the battle for Jerusalem, he was awarded three flints from the Church of the Holy Sepulcher. Each year these flints light a "holy fire" to cleanse the crowd, much as Dante's purifying flames of Purgatory rinsed away sins before entering Paradise.

The boys can't see a thing with all the people jammed so tightly, so I tell them to sneak through the crowd. Katy panics that we'll never see them again, but I assure her that they know to meet for gelato afterward. The crowd sways and pushes toward the sacred cart drawn by white oxen covered in flowers. From inside the cathedral, a fake dove rigged up to a long wire is lit up with bottle rockets and zips out into the square. The cart, heavy with gunpowder and fireworks, shoots up every type of explosive, pinwheel, and sparkler that can fit. Smoke fills the square and reduces visibility. The deafening bells from Giotto's campanile bong incessantly as we retreat to the *gelateria* in search of the boys, hoping that our sins have been wiped away from the holy fire as we cough and gasp for fresh air.

Katy breathes a sigh of relief as Eilif and Otto are waiting patiently for us. They know that when we get back to the apartment, they'll get some treats sent from their adopted *nonna* in Modena: giant chocolate eggs as big as their heads.

I SUPPOSE we shouldn't be surprised that many of the holidays and parties revolve around fantastic food. Eilif is invited to his classmate Sasha's birthday party held at their school, and the father is the owner of the restaurant across the street from our apartment. By this time, Katy has gotten used to the late-night noise down on the street from the merrymakers exiting his *ristorante.* When we arrive at the party, two large tables sag from the mounds of delicious cuisine and chilled bottles on the table. Sasha's father Tommaso greets us with a glass of fizzy Prosecco as we are the only guests. "I thought the party was at four o'clock," I say, a bit embarrassed.

He assures me that we're not too early. Tommaso says he wanted to make it as easy as possible on the guests. "We don't say that the birthday is *at* four but that it's *from* four. We will be here, so people can show up whenever they want. We want people to be relaxed." We take a sip of the white wine, then gulp when he adds, "People will start arriving at five thirty or six."

Even if this is a birthday for a ten-year-old boy, we eat local pecorino and stracciatella cheese. The kids go right for the mini pizzas and *bomboloni,* or "big bombs," a sort of Tuscan donut. The rest of the guests show up long after us and an immaculate red Alfa Romeo spider zooms into the courtyard. Blue smoke puffs out of the exhaust pipe, filling the courtyard with a smell that means power.

Ten kids pile inside the tiny convertible and trod over the pristine leather seats with their grubby shoes as the owner laughs. Apparently, this is the ride for the birthday boy. Who

needs car seats or even seatbelts? The parents wave happily as he revs the growling 120 horsepower engine. I cover my eyes and imagine the kids tumbling off the back of the car as he accelerates. I'm worried we're going to be hauling some of them off to the hospital, or maybe to the herbalist instead. I peek to see if our boys are in the car and for once am relieved to discover them throwing basketballs at each other. Thankfully they aren't such thrill seekers as the Florentines. In the meantime, someone wisely shuts the gate and the Alfa Romeo can only do donuts around the gravel parking lot.

## MEAT ON THE STREET

A proud Florentine mother who has also lived in the United States tells me that Italians treat their kids differently. "American parents at the beach are always right there with their children down on their hands and knees making enormous sandcastles and the kids are constantly having fits. The Italian parents, meanwhile, are suntanning and ignoring their kids who are running around free." She says that Italian kids are just a little more intelligent and "with it." Her American husband scoffs and the other Italian parents roll their eyes. One parent from a different region teases her that soon she'll say that the children from Florence are even smarter than those from other Italian cities. "It could be . . ." she says, without a hint of irony.

Despite her pride, she's on to something. Italian kids are more used to fending for themselves and living in an adult world. Sitting at the table in a restaurant for a couple of hours—an impossibility for most American kids—is normal. I've never seen an Italian "children's menu," although waiters often dote on our kids. Perhaps they give them too much leeway since they offer them plain pasta with butter rather than pushing them to taste Tuscan cuisine.

With the American university students who just arrived, I push them as well to fit in and try the local food. I beg them to steer clear of "American breakfast" and hamburgers. The students are generally open to the experiences—on their own terms. The waitress asks one of the students if she'd like a cappuccino. "Actually, could I get a latte?" she responds.

The waitress is a bit confused: "*Va bene*. Hot or cold?"

"Oh definitely an iced latte," the thrilled student says. She gives me a smirk since I'd told the class that Italians don't use much ice since they think it hurts the liver. I stop the waitress since she was about to bring the student a glass of cold milk, or "*latte*."

Another student brings her own bottle of "French" dressing with her into restaurants to liven up her salads. The waiters don't raise an eyebrow, probably because she looks like the voluptuous movie star Anita Ekberg out of *La Dolce Vita*.

Another student regrets not bringing ranch dressing, mostly because she likes to dip her pizza in it. "I love to put ranch dressing on mac and cheese, but it might be good on their pasta too." I shudder to think what the waiters would think of that.

A student named Natasha orders a ham and mushroom pizza but tells me that the dough is difficult for her to digest. She picks all the toppings off and eats them without touching the crust. "Is something the matter?" the waiter wonders.

"No, no. It's great," she says happily.

The students look over a menu that has some specialties from Rome. One of them asks the waiter about *coda alla vaccinara*. The waiter doesn't know the English words, so he mimes something coming out of his rear and gestures how delicious it is. The students look at me wondering if this is a joke. I explain that it's oxtail. The waiter instead recommends the pasta with *pajata.*

"What's that?" Paola asks.

The waiter says you start with a *vitello.*

"Baby cow? For cute!"

Then he mimes that they rip out the intestines and cook it up. "*Buonissimo!*"

The students are horrified and mostly opt for vegetarian dishes.

A student from Nebraska, Kelly, asks the poor waiter for chocolate milk to go with her pasta. The waiter can't understand, so he asks Sabrina, the Italian guide for the group. She doesn't understand what this is either, so she asks the student for clarification. Kelly explains, "You know, milk with chocolate syrup inside."

The waiter and Sabrina laugh, assuming she must be joking. When they realize she's not, the waiter shakes his finger indignantly and chides, "I could make you this milk with chocolate with your pasta, but I won't, for your sake."

I take the students on a field trip to the market in Florence to taste the cheeses, salamis, and prosciutto. They avoid the stand run by the guy with a calendar of a nude pinup girl with breasts bigger than her head. The man doesn't mind that none of them shop there. He's busy scoping out the stockinged legs of the passing women.

We travel to the Adriatic in Le Marche, so I use our budget for a fabulous seafood lunch. I realize the students are used to their food batter-fried, so seeing clams and mussels doesn't compute. Pulling bones off of small sardines and anchovies fresh out of the sea is too complicated. "I just don't eat any meat with bones. It freaks me out," one of the students confesses. When she sees shrimp with all the little legs that need to be peeled off, she is overwhelmed.

I feel guilty for pushing them too far, but they assure me they'll still be adventurous. When we spend a day in Padova, I point out horse meat tartare on the menu. "Let's try it!" Alice says. "When else are we ever going to get raw horse meat?" I'm impressed that most of the students take a bite.

"Mmm, it's actually delicious," a student declares.

We take a one-day field trip and visit the official balsamic vinegar testing area in the city hall of Modena. The head of the vinegar consortium puts his ceremonial medal around his neck and he's now ready to begin. He patiently explains the difference between a three-dollar commercial grade vinegar and the traditional balsamic in a bottle conceived by the car stylist Giugiaro that can easily cost $200.

"This is more expensive than heroin!" Natasha exclaims. I'm not sure how she knows the price of this drug.

". . . and even more addictive," her friend adds.

Several of the students purchase a bottle of the expensive elixir, but Natasha confesses, "I have no idea how to use this at home, but it looks so good!" It's no wonder that fifty billion euros a year are spent in restaurants in Italy.

After Katy's and my experience living in Modena, the "culinary capital of Italy," she isn't sure how the food is going to stack up in Florence but is sure the artwork will make up for it. "I want to live in Florence but eat like a Modenese," she tells me.

Over the weekend, we take the train back to Modena and tell *la nonna,* our adopted Modenese grandmother, that we'll already have eaten at our friend Marina's house after we meet our friend Guido for a late morning coffee. She is obviously a bit upset we didn't choose her first and replies, "Well, you can't have two lunches!" she advises.

"Why not?" Eilif wonders.

Instead, we suggest an early dinner before getting back on the train. This way we could squeeze in two delicious meals. She doesn't understand the idea of having an early dinner at five thirty or six. That's just not done. Instead, we arrive at her house at three thirty, after a lengthy lunch at Marina's. *La nonna* puts three large pieces of different cakes on the table that I assume will be split between the five of us. Instead, we each get a giant cake plate followed by strawberries and ice cream and a bowl of cherries. When it's time to leave, she recommends we pack a sandwich in case we're still hungry.

The next weekend, our friend Giovanni from Milano visits us in Florence. He sees the group of American students and asks, "You got ten women to travel with you to Italy? How did you do that?" I insist it's not like that. Besides, there are two male students on the trip. "Oh, then it's Eric and his twelve apostles," he teases.

Giovanni sniffs the air of Florence and notices, "*C'è un odore di carne sulle strade*" (there's a smell of meat on the streets). The famous Florentine beefsteak is being grilled in restaurants across town—no wonder the dogs go crazy here. In front of the Medici Chapel, we see a butcher hauling over his shoulder two giant flanks of beef that drip blood on his white smock.

Eilif notices all the photo menus around the tourist streets with two-inch thick cuts of beef. "So when is it that we're going to eat a *bistecca alla fiorentina*?" he asks. He feels it's his duty to eat one of these oversized steaks, so we take him out to the Trattoria Casalinga near our apartment to see what he can do.

When the waitress sets down a two-pound steak in front of him, he asks, "What's the red liquid around it? Is it blood?"

We tell him it's just meat juice.

"Hmmm. I think I want to become a vegetarian."

Fortunately, the steak is succulent. He decides now is not the time to give up meat.

THE OTHER FLORENTINE DELICACY is gelato. The Medici claim to have commissioned the first real ice cream, and then Caterina de' Medici whisked off the best chefs to France with her to make the delicacy for her marriage to the future king. Sicily had something similar: desserts made with the snows of Mount Etna. The emperor Nero had his icy treats, and even Marco Polo supposedly brought back a secret gelato recipe from China. However, to cement its claim in the popular consciousness, Florence now hosts the annual Gelato Festival, and Tuscans consistently win the contest for the best gelato in Italy.

One afternoon, we take the students to the fairgrounds. Each of them have a card for six tastes plus a "gelato cocktail." For once, they can't even eat all the gelato put in front of them. That evening, though, a few of them are searching for more.

Everyone has their favorite *gelateria* that makes their own "artisanal" ice cream. Katy says that one of the reasons she loves Italy is that she can get into a heated discussion with our landlady Fede about where to get the best pizza and gelato in town. These arguments typically end with the concession of "Yes, it's all a matter of personal taste. If you like it, that's what's important." However, there is a bit of questioning of the other's taste, and then a good excuse to sneak out to the rival *gelateria* to give it another try.

The American students can't wait to have their morning *gelato,* and our Italian guide Sabrina is amazed. "We never eat gelato in the morning and then usually only on weekends."

"Then why are the ice cream stores open in the morning," one of the students asks. Sabrina doesn't know and several students load up. I tell them we're on our way to eat soon, but they can't resist a second gelato right before lunch.

"This is just a warm-up!" a student warns.

At the restaurant across from our apartment run by the father of Eilif's classmate, I encourage the students to try the homemade pasta, but Natasha admits, "I have a hard time digesting carbohydrates" and orders a large cheese plate in hopes that will go down more easily. She's upset that the restaurant is out of profiteroles for dessert and announces, "I guess I'll just have to settle for the tiramisù." The waiter brings a giant portion, which she finishes handily. "How can the Italians eat like this and not gain weight?"

I later tell Giovanni about these students, as I'm worried that our kids will pick up these indulgent eating habits. He looks at me as if I've become a food snob wanting to be more Italian than the Italians. Giovanni proclaims that gelato is so good that it's fine to eat it anytime. "Anyone who says otherwise is fooling themselves." He then treats us to a delicious cone at the famous *gelateria* that's called "*Perché no?*" (Why not?)

One of the students is so moved by her experience abroad that she declares, "This is life changing." I'm so pleased that Italy has made such an impression.

She corrects me, "Oh, I was only talking about the caffè macchiato that changed my life."

# DEADBEAT DAD

I try to follow Giovanni's advice to avoid judging my fellow countrymen so harshly. He reminds me of when I first came to Italy and made all sorts of cultural blunders. He reminisces about when I made the—apparently terrible—mistake of making tomato sauce with both basil and oregano.

I try to accept that my college students view Rome through the eyes of the *Lizzie McGuire Movie*. It isn't the Trevi Fountain, but "this is where Lizzie met Paolo!" It isn't a cool red Vespa, but "Lizzie took Paolo around on one just like that!" Originally, I was worried about having our little kids along on field trips with the university students, but now I think they'll fit right in. Besides, the students like to have little translators.

I should be glad the students ask so many questions, but I often don't have the answers. A student asks me, "Why is that building painted yellow?" I'm stumped.

Another wonders, "Is that manure over there?" when we're near the Colosseum. "If so where are the horses? They must have brought them in to help fertilize, right?"

Fortunately, our guide, Sabrina, can clarify these important issues. Her patience with the students' barrage of questions is remarkable. We arrange to meet at the cathedral at noon and a student asks seriously, "In front or on top?"

I tell Sabrina that the one thing I love about Italians is that they usually don't tell others what to do. Or at least they know it's rude to be pushy and to force others to obey the rules, as they wouldn't want anyone to do that to them. I find that I'm far more critical of my fellow countrymen's behavior than Italians are. They seem to be much more accepting that people do things differently.

Sabrina does step in, however, when a business student gives a report on Italian business to the other students: "The crazy thing with Italy is that if you get caught for doing something illegal, you just bribe the judge. That's how you do it!" Sabrina gently corrects her that this is still unlawful.

Sabrina seems to know what the students are going to do before it happens. I want to give them a shot of espresso at the end of the meal, but Sabrina warns, "Careful. Then they'll want cappuccino or *caffelatte,* and we'll be here another half hour."

She's unflappable, except for when I mention to the students that Florence is very different from Naples and southern Italy. "Northerners say that southern Italy is like Africa, and southerners say that the north is Germany," I say. "Florence is just a little closer to Germany."

"Perhaps," Sabrina clarifies, "but we are *not* German!"

Our other guide for the day, Francesca, confirms that they are not even close to being German. However, there is a strange connection with the Germans because of the historic bridge, Ponte Vecchio. Francesca explains that when Hitler visited the city in 1938, he wanted to cross the bridge, but "if Hitler would have walked on the bridge with the normal Italians, he would have been punched and stabbed." Instead, he went up above it, across the skyway called the Vasari Corridor. Mussolini had even expanded for his German guest the skyway's windows, now dubbed the "Hitler windows" by the Florentines. The students are paying attention now, but they question Francesca's judgment when she says, "In fact, the only thing Mussolini really did wrong was to become friends with Hitler."

I like that students see everything with new eyes and not necessarily as the art books say they should. Susan wants to sneak a photo of Michelangelo's *David* that isn't too scandalous. She walks around the nude sculpture to get an inconspicuous angle but is disturbed that she can't cover up that he's naked and, well, gorgeous.

Kelly, the student from Nebraska, tries to make sense of all of the paintings of tortured saints. I explain a scene of St. Catherine of Alexandria, who is stripped naked and put on a giant wooden wheel so she is crushed as it rolls downhill.

"Golly!" Kelly exclaims. "Is that really necessary?"

"Of course!" interjects her classmate John. "All of them had to be martyred in some terrible way, otherwise they wouldn't be true saints."

We move on to a suggestive painting of Jesus and Mary Magdalene. Kelly ponders, "It was typical for guys to be married back then, most of the apostles were, and then they started following Jesus. I'll bet that he was married too and then went off to preach."

"Are you saying that Jesus was a deadbeat dad?" I tease.

"Oh! I wouldn't say it like that!" She thinks about it, then wonders aloud, "but I guess he was . . ."

---

One day when our group meets to tour Florence, the two male students show up in T-shirts and khaki shorts when the temperature rises to fifty degrees Fahrenheit. "I think we stand out a little," John says, after noticing the Italians still in parkas and scarves with winter boots. I try not to judge as the guards at the churches are harsher than I am. No one will allow them to enter with their disrespectful knees bared or the women with a scandalous shoulder exposed.

I reassure them that they aren't so bad compared to the drunk tourist who climbed on the statue of Neptune in Florence and broke off the hand and trident of the god of the sea. Thankfully, my students are well behaved. One of them is shocked by a tourist from eastern Europe as they climb up Giotto's bell tower. The dizzying spiral staircase probably made the tourist nauseous, so she vomited into her own hands. Afterward, the student tells us that the tourist then lost the rest of her lunch into her purse. Everyone was disgusted, but the tourist just shrugged and kept going to the top with her handbag dripping all the way. For the next two days, we saw the poor tourist around Florence and other students teased the student that "There's your barf-buddy . . . your puke-pal . . . your upchuck *amica.*"

Despite all the tourists in Florence, I encourage the students to visit the fantastic sites here in Tuscany, but they take any chance to leave town. "Since I'm here," they tell me, "this weekend I'm going to . . ." I expect to hear Pisa, Siena, or another nearby hill town. Instead, Mary is going to Spain, Darcy is traveling to Austria, and Kathryn is off to Tel Aviv.

"Israel? That's not even the same continent," I respond.

"Yeah," Kathryn responds, "but I just thought I'd take advantage of my time over here."

"You realize that Israel is more than two thousand miles away, right?"

She's unfazed that she has to travel two hours on the train and an hour on the bus just to get to her flight from Milan. "The cheapest flight I found leaves at 7 a.m., so I'll sleep in the airport beforehand." The students spend most of their weekends traveling and are exhausted by the time class starts on Monday.

Now as our time is in Florence is coming to an end, I ask them about the Italians they've met. Mary says that she saw a cute Italian guy that she wanted to talk to, but she could only remember one Italian word from class. To spark a conversation, she tried out her word when she saw him on the street: "*Arrivederci!*"

He walked away.

Despite the confusion, I encourage the students to keep trying with their Italian. After six weeks here in Italy, I overhear Kelly cheerfully thanking the receptionist at a hotel, "*Grazia!*"

He politely corrects her, "I am not '*Grazia*,' that is a name of a woman. I think you mean '*grazie*,' right?"

John, on the other hand, tells me that during his month and a half in Florence, "I haven't really spoken with any Italians, and the only Italian I've learned is *sì*."

I console myself by hearing that he had a great time, whereas nothing seemed to go right for many of them. I take a group to arguably the most beautiful city in the world: Venice. They walk out of the station, and one of the students has her mouth open for a couple of minutes as she is rendered speechless that this place exists. Another student doesn't understand what the big deal is. I tell her to look at the gondolas, the bridges, the palaces on the glittering canal . . . She admits, "Well, I did forget my glasses in the hotel, so everything is kind of blurry."

Afterward, I ask Natasha how her trip to Venice was and she shrugs. "Well, Venice is overrated. It's kind of lame."

"Really? Venice is lame?" I respond in disbelief.

"Yeah, and that glass factory is a joke."

After comments such as this, I assume that many of the students would be glad to go home. Instead, they have Italian-themed parties at home with food they snuck through customs. Natasha declares, "It was the best two weeks of my life," and Anna wants to change her major just so she can come back to Italy.

To prove to our kids that Venice isn't "lame," Katy and I take the family up to this watery city. We exit the train station and Otto proclaims that Venice is his dreamland. Astri sees a gondola and claims it as "Mine!" Even with the many tourists, Venice is ideal for kids as no scooters or cars threaten to run them down. The only danger is falling into the canal. We wander through the labyrinth of streets unconcerned if we get lost because the kids mostly want to clap to scare up the flocks of pigeons.

We jump on *vaporetto* #1 that takes us by water up the Grand Canal back to the train station after our visit. Astri finally has her own boat, and we squeeze out on the open-air deck in the back for the best view as the sun sets. The passengers on the gondolas and other boats greet us across the water because who can resist the vigorous waving of an excited three-year-old girl? She hangs precariously off the back as I hang on to her hood in case she falls. When we reach the station, I explain that we need to get on our train. She looks out on the canal with all the sleek black boats skimming over the waves made red by the sunset and says, "Bye-bye! Bye-bye!" I wonder when I'll be back in this fantasyland with her and the family, and if she'll remember anything.

## LOVE IS ALL AROUND

Katy said that when we lived in Italy fourteen years before, she always dreamed of returning here someday with kids. Now here we are rushing out the door early each school day. We walk two kilometers across Florence's historic center just to bring the boys to school. As we approach the Ponte Santa Trinità, I put on my professor hat and point out that this is where Dante saw his beloved Beatrice. The kids are more interested in the tourists who have already discovered gelato this early.

I point out the fog enveloping the bridge from the River Arno, but this haze instead rises from a gaggle of junior high kids, all smoking and flirting out of sight of their parents and teachers. We stop for a moment on the bridge to watch the sun rise and poke through the arches of the spectacular, precarious Ponte Vecchio. I now remember why we came to Italy.

I look down to see some lovers have climbed over the railing of the bridge to make out on the dangerous precipice just a foot away from a terrible fall into the swift current sixty feet below. I point out the death-defying lovers to Katy and tell her, "That doesn't seem like such a good idea, but I'd go there with you."

"Oh, isn't that sweet," she says sarcastically. I look at her for an explanation, so she adds, "Did you notice he also has his hand down her pants?"

As we walk through this Renaissance city, I avoid calling attention to the twenty-four-hour cigarette machines and the condom vending machines outside the pharmacies. We pass the Ospedale di Bonifacio from 1377 that became a "hospital for the incurable" in the sixteenth century for patients who had "the French disease," or syphilis, so called because French troops brought the bacteria with them during an invasion of Naples. The building later became an insane asylum and is now the *questura*, or police headquarters. While the boys read the sign, I avoid explaining syphilis and all the terrible medieval cures for these poor people who then probably did go insane and were locked up here.

I also dodge Otto's question, "Who are those women that are always there?" He points to a hotel where each morning a group of suggestively dressed women in high heels and too

much makeup gather to smoke cigarettes and then go home after a long night.

On the other hand, we watch a lovely foreign couple who have traveled all the way to Florence to get married in an elaborate ceremony in this city of lovers. Photographers follow the bride dressed in traditional white and the groom in a stiff tuxedo through the piazzas to chronicle every moment of their visit.

Love is in the air, and Eilif complains that the other kids in his fourth-grade class pester him about who his girlfriend is. "How can I have a girlfriend if we are only going to be here three months?"

"Well, it's not like you have to marry her," Katy replies.

He obviously doesn't want a girlfriend and is upset with his new best friend at school who tells him, "I'm in love! Isn't that great? I'm sorry Eilif, but at recess, I need to be with my true love. You should be happy for me!"

Eilif has to find other friends, but a week later, his best friend is back playing with him. We ask Eilif what happened. "Oh, he said that they just needed some time apart."

After we drop the boys off at school each morning, Astri is exhausted and ready for her morning nap. Rather than sleep in the stroller, however, she often cries the two kilometers home. When she hollers going down the narrow alleyways, sometimes store clerks will bring a cookie out to settle down our little sweetheart—anything to stop her wailing. Astri then gives me a knowing smirk as if she planned this all along.

Katy says, "Now that we're here with children, I dream of the days we were in Italy alone." Still, Astri does her job in this romantic city: Her screams wake up young lovers from their reveries as a reminder to either use birth control or be ready for the results of their midnight trysts.

AT THE BEGINNING of our three months in Italy, the boys asked, "Aren't we going home soon?" Now that it's time for us to return to the United States, they want to stay. One of my students is distraught at having to return to the States. She asks, "How can I exist in my homeland now that I know such a place exists?"

Being in Italy, something clicks with Astri and she realizes that speaking Italian is fun. She uses dramatic hand gestures and adds a lilt to her Italian as if she's making fun of it. Our Italian friends are pleased that she's finally catching on.

Otto, on the other hand, is sick of speaking Italian and starts talking to me in English. I pretend not to understand. Eilif is horrified by Otto: "What are you doing? Don't you know that now you know a whole 'nother language?" Years later, Otto aces the AP Italian test.

Eilif is sad and worried that he'll eventually lose his Italian when we leave Italy. "Papà, so I don't forget it, will you always speak Italian to me?"

"Wow, you must be proud," Katy congratulates me. Then she whispers, "Notice, though, that this is all because he's too lazy to pick up a book to read in Italian!" At least he realizes the value of knowing a second language. I'll take it.

It's the first of June and we've surpassed our ninety days in Italy. The heat is already unbearable in Florence. We haul our mound of luggage down three flights of steps to the entrance of our apartment. We have to hail two cabs to fit everything.

Our bags are stuffed with truffled wild boar salami that the butcher in the Florence market said was safe to bring to the United States. I notice in the airport duty-free shop they are selling prosciutto, so I ask the cashier if we can legally bring this back to the United States. "No, the laws still say you can't bring it in," she informs me.

"Well, why are you selling it?" I ask.

"You just have to hide it really well in your luggage, and you might be able to get it in."

"But isn't that smuggling?"

She shrugs. "That's the risk you take for good food."

In the airport in Minneapolis, we tell the agents that we have salami, but the butcher in Florence told us that we could bring it. The customs agent laughs, confiscates the salami, and throws it all away.

An Italian behind us in line is appalled. "At least in Chicago or New York they sneak it home to eat it. What a waste!" Our last taste of Italy is in the trash.

# PART III

# Bringing It All Back Home

## *DOLCE FAR NIENTE*

After returning from Florence, I remind the kids about the Italian concept of *dolce far niente*, or how sweet it is to do nothing. Relaxing is the best reward of all. We need to bring this easy living back home with us.

Astri doesn't believe me and probably thinks this is just another ploy to brainwash her. She studies Katy and me since we're always busy doing something and asking her not to interrupt when we're talking on the phone. Astri recognizes cell phones are power. I tell her it's naptime; she grabs a calculator on her desk and narrates as she types into the keypad. "Grandma! Papà is bossing me around. I don't want to take a nap!"

Katy and I are exhausted after returning from Italy, so we set the clocks earlier to try to get the kids to bed. We forgot they'll also wake up earlier. We tell them it's daylight savings time, so they need to go back to sleep. Otto researches daylight savings time and wakes us up extra early just to prove us wrong.

"Otto never seems to need us as parents," Katy points out. "At least Eilif pretends to and Astri needs us *all* the time. Otto, though, it was like he looked at us and said, 'That's OK. No thanks.'"

Otto's self-determination makes him stressed. He takes up the bassoon and asks me, "Do you prefer the Berlin or Vienna Philharmonic?"

Katy advises him against being a perfectionist, and he should lower his standards to relax. Otto is appalled: "If I have to be just average, what's the point of living?" I can't help but think he's talking about us.

Eilif, on the other hand, loves the idea of *dolce far niente.* He hangs a sign he brought back from a hotel in Italy on his door handle that says "*Si prega di non disturbare*" or "Do Not Disturb." He thinks this entitles him to do nothing.

When he leaves his room, he turns over the sign to read "*Si prega di rifare la camera,*" which is translated below in English as "Maid: Please Make Up This Room As Soon As Possible." Katy is not pleased.

We tell Eilif he needs to help out more around the house. He replies that *dolce far niente* is all about not doing anything. He's got me, but I explain it's only sweet to do nothing after you've finished all your work. He's not buying it and argues we always have more work for him to do.

I should be pleased Eilif is arguing in Italian and clearly smarter than I am. To get him to do some chores, I ask him directly: "Can you help set the table?"

"No, *grazie!*" he responds politely.

"No, really, could you please help out?"

"That's OK. Thanks!"

I try a different tack and let him choose: "Do you want to help make dinner or clean up afterwards?"

Eilif recognizes this is a false choice: "Neither."

I complain to Katy that Eilif won't help out. Eilif defends himself: "He asked me if I *wanted* to help, and I don't *want* to. I'm being truthful! Do you want me to lie?"

"Well, how can I get you to help?" I ask.

"You have to *tell* me to do it."

"Really? You want me to order you around?"

"*Sì!*"

"OK. Set the table!"

"God! You're so mean!" He storms off to his room, slams the door, and hangs the "Do Not Disturb" sign on the handle. He has truly learned how to argue like an Italian to get his way.

I ASPIRE TO HAVE a perfectly clean Italian apartment like our friends in Italy. Now that we're back, though, our house is turned upside down.

I want to bring that tidiness home. Perhaps we could host an Italian exchange student as impetus. Sheila, the librarian in Climax, Minnesota, tells me that she hosted an exchange student from Bologna for a year, but Valentina expected to practice *dolce far niente.* She had no interest in chores. "I picked her up at the airport in Grand Forks in the evening," Sheila told me. "We drove for miles in the darkness away from the lights. Valentina started getting very nervous. We finally saw the lights of the small town of Ada. She couldn't believe people lived in these shacks and said they should all be bulldozed except for maybe the red stone courthouse in Ada from 1904."

"How did she like your house?" I ask.

"She looked around and asked, 'When is the maid coming?'

We had just repainted and cleaned everything! She had standards."

"How did you get her to help out?" I ask, hoping for some tips.

"We all took turns doing the dishes after supper—me, my spouse, and our eight-year-old child. Then we told Valentina that it was her turn to wash the dishes. She protested that she had never washed dishes before in her life. We explained how you wash, rinse, and then set the plates to dry. She did it, but we noticed she was bent over the sink, sobbing that she had been lowered to such a level. To make her feel better, we eventually took her to the 'big city' of Fargo so she could buy expensive jeans at the mall with her grandparent's Visa Gold card."

Perhaps we could hold out a carrot for our kids if they finish their chores, but Katy won't hear of it. "Why do we always have to reward the kids?" Astri finishes her twenty-page book on counting and there's a certificate of completion. Really?

At Astri's elementary school, the kids are encouraged to walk or bike to school. The reward is hot cocoa and ice cream sandwiches. Katy is outraged, "I thought they were supposed to be getting in shape!"

One day she brings the boys to school late because they had a dentist appointment. The school receptionist gives them each a lollipop. "What? They get a sucker for being late?"

I wonder, "Maybe it's because they had actually had an excuse and didn't just skip school."

She asks, "What do they get if they're on time?"

My parents want to bring all the grandkids to Annie's Parlour for hamburgers and malts, so I use this meal as a reward for when they've finished their chores. Eilif plays the piano instead.

With only a half hour before they leave, I ask Eilif if he's done his work. He approaches Katy and declares, "Papà said I can't go to Annie's because I didn't do my work."

I tell Eilif that I do want him to go but still want him to do his chores.

"Oh, so you want me to go and eat French fries and hamburgers rather than do my work?"

I respond, "Well, I want you to keep your commitment to them because I care about other people."

"Oh, so you care about other people and not the work?"

"Yes, Eilif, I do care about them."

"You care about other people? Then when do think about me? Never?"

Otto takes Eilif's lead on chore evasion, opting for philosophical questioning of why the job must be done in the first place. I suppose this is the essence of *dolce far niente.* Katy and I ask Otto to cut the grass, but he contemplates, "Maybe we should just let our lawn grow super tall like those lazy farmers with the tall grass in their fields."

"Umm, those are crops, Otto."

He chooses a new tack: "You're not the boss of me!"

Astri interrupts, "Who is then?"

"Me!" Otto responds. "Just like you are the boss of you."

Astri protests, "No! I'm not the boss of me. I'm the boss of everyone!"

To avoid a power struggle of ordering the kids to work or doling out rewards, I imagine that they'll help if I entrust them with a task. The boys learned how to use euros in Italy to buy gelato and Pokémon cards, so now I give Eilif some money to go to the Longfellow Market to buy some bread for lunch. He and Astri walk up there happily and return with the groceries. I'm pleased that I finally get them to help out.

Afterward, Eilif gives me the change: "Yeah, I don't know why it was so expensive." I look at the receipt that lists "sprinkle cake donuts."

"What?" Eilif asks. "Why is that on the receipt? I never got donuts! I'm mad now."

I say nothing.

# DESTRUCTO-DOG

Our dog Bacco is thrilled that we're home from Italy. I don't dare tell anyone that it's been rather nice not taking care of a dog for three months. Everything is cleaner and there's no fur on our clothes.

Katy pets Bacco and asks, "Who's my favorite dog? You are!"

Astri can't believe it. "What? You like Bacco better than me?"

"Are you a dog?" Katy asks. Still, when the kids question us who our favorite child is, we always keep them guessing. A bit of competition keeps them in line.

The kids haven't absorbed that we are actually back home. One evening, we watch the film *Babe* and the kids see the black-and-white border collies. "Aww! We want a dog!" Astri squeals.

Katy responds: "You have one just like in the movie. He's lying at your feet."

When we bring the kids in for their checkups, our family doctor tells us it's good to let the kids play in the mud to build up their resistance. Why should they bathe at all if dirt is good for them? What's the point of cleaning the house? We can just use the same dirty old sponges and bath toys and encourage Bacco to lick the kids clean.

We don't dare follow the doctor's orders. Katy asks Astri to wash her hands and face after eating and before touching the sofa. "It's OK, mom, I licked my hands." I look over to see the dog licking her as well. Astri holds up her hands, "All clean!"

SOMETIME AFTER WE RETURN from Italy, Bacco dies. We bury him in the backyard. We mourn for weeks. Despite my complaining, I know what a loyal companion we had. I wanted to be adventurous and show the kids that Italy and the world could be their home. Instead, everyone else recognized that home is where the dog is.

Katy wants another Australian shepherd right away, but I argue that we can't replace Bacco. I also wouldn't mind returning to Italy and don't want to worry about a dog.

Instead, we go to the zoo to look at the animals. Eilif is disappointed that they don't have his favorite animal: the crow.

Astri is upset too. "They don't have dogs? Why not? What about kitty cats?"

Conversations always return to dogs. Soon we drive two hours to view a newborn batch of nine Australian shepherds. I know that once we see these puppies it's impossible to come back empty-handed.

Named for the Harry Nilsson song, little Arrow the blue merle Australian shepherd joins our family. Arrow seems dumber than Bacco, but more content. He stands on his hind legs and eats raspberries like a bear. Katy wonders, "Maybe that's what we should have done with our kids to make them happier: Feed them chips of lead paint."

Katy brings Arrow to Petco to buy puppy food, but he bolts in the store when he's frightened by a big dog. The gates come down to prevent him from escaping and the staff search for him.

Even though "he's the cutest puppy ever," as Astri notes, he's earned the nickname "Destructo-Dog." He chews everything: chairs, table legs, Astri's hairbrush and binders, even Otto's retainer, which—incredibly—was covered by insurance. I worry that he's going to swallow Otto's socks like the dog I read about that had his stomach pumped because he ate forty-three socks.

The mother of Astri's friend tells us that we're lucky because her golden retriever puppy "eats our walls!"

Arrow always wants to be with us, so we tie him to the front stoop so he can join us in the front yard. He eats the welcome mat. He eats his bowl, stuffed animals, his poop, rabbit poop. Then he eats matches and is violently ill for four days. Katy calls this the "matchstick diet" since Arrow has slimmed down.

Arrow responds to the world by taste. Katy warns guests that "Arrow has tasted everything at his level, so anything below three feet is a little wet."

When we bring him to the veterinarian, he licks the walls, the door, everything. The vet says, "I know his type. He can't hold his licker!"

Arrow continues eating everything. Even Jesus Christ, or rather a floating rubber ducky made to look like Jesus. Eilif wonders, "Hasn't Jesus suffered enough? I mean they nailed him to a cross and now the dog eats him?"

Otto rationalizes: "Well, 'dog' is 'god' backwards."

Eilif proclaims, "Maybe Arrow is Christian since he's eating the body of Christ!"

WHEN SUMMER COMES, Katy and I drive Astri to Camp Warren while the boys stay home with the dog. We receive a cryptic message from Otto: "The dog chewed up Astri's wallet." Astri had just counted her money—almost ninety dollars from gifts over the years.

We text back asking if the dog actually ate the money. The boys don't respond. I write again telling them to gather the money and we'll tape the bills back together. No answer.

We return home late after a rainstorm. I take out the recycling and notice the backyard is covered with partially chewed bills. Five dollars here, twenty dollars there. The boys say they got distracted and just never got around to picking it up.

Arrow recognizes what is important to us and wants to eat it. Strangely, his favorite place to lie is under the trampoline on top of Bacco's grave. Is he channeling Bacco's ghost? One hot day Arrow starts digging down at the spot, but only gets down about six inches before, thankfully, giving up.

Arrow tilts his head when we speak to try to understand both English and Italian. "*Vuoi mangiare?*" I ask. He salivates. "*Passeggiata?*" I ask, and he goes to the door ready for a walk. The dog learns Italian faster than the kids.

We joke that Arrow wants to be human. He likes to sit on a chair at the table like he's one of us.

One morning, he has something in his mouth and dutifully drops it. Out comes a magnetic word tile that we had on the refrigerator with just one word on it: "boy." We're stunned. He's our canine Pinocchio who wants to be human.

## ARE WE REAL?

Astri is pretending and Eilif doesn't like it.

We've been reading *Pinocchio, La Befana,* and other stories so her imagination is running wild. She has her foot in two worlds, the Italian and the English, as she remembers the masks and the make-believe of the *Commedia dell'arte.*

In Italy, we gave her some euros to buy candy and she realized the power of money. Now she asks her brother for fourteen dollars for imaginary ice cream. Eilif, who is seven years older, feels it's his duty as a responsible sibling to play with her since we're always encouraging him to do so. He gets his wallet and angrily counts out fourteen dollars for her. She doesn't want actual money but pretend money for pretend ice cream.

Astri licks the fake ice cream and fantasizes she's a dog. She asks Eilif what kind of animal he wants to be. "A homo sapien," he replies stoically.

"No, no, no! What *animal*?" Astri demands.

"That *is* an animal, Astri. You are a homo sapien too."

"No, I'm not! Mom! Eilif's being mean!" Astri insists that she is Bat Dog and won't respond unless we call her "Ace."

Eilif won't stand for this and argues against the logic of a preschooler. "No, your name is 'Astri.'"

Astri shows Eilif that she has a cape and even a name tag on a string that says "Ace."

Eilif is disturbed by her detachment from reality: "No, you are 'Astri,' and I can even prove it by finding your birth certificate!" Even though Eilif constantly wore costumes when he was younger, he needs Astri to understand: "Superheroes are not real. They are fake people in imaginary costumes that try to save the world. They do not exist."

Otto interrupts, "Well, they do 'exist,' at least in our minds. They are stories, right?"

"I guess so . . ." Eilif reluctantly agrees, but he's clearly concerned Otto is leading their little sister astray.

Astri doesn't care that they are all made-up. She wants her brothers to play dress-up in their old, painfully small superhero costumes. Katy reminds Eilif of how much his sister looks up to him: "With great power comes great responsibility!"

Eilif recognizes the quote: "That's what Peter Parker's uncle said to him before he had superpowers and found out he was Spider-Man!" Never mind that she's quoting Winston Churchill.

Katy bribes Eilif with five dollars so he squeezes into his old Superman costume and comes with us to the co-op. He agrees and Astri is thrilled. In the cereal aisle, Eilif runs into two of his classmates. He's not a bit embarrassed that he's dressed in a skintight Superman outfit with pads to make him look like a steroid-popping bodybuilder. Without a bit of sarcasm, one of them comments, "Nice costume, Eilif!"

I'm exhausted from traveling and raising kids, and now Christmas is coming. I collapse on the couch and ask Eilif a

question entirely in English. He stares at me dumbfounded. "*Cosa fai?*" "What are you doing?"

What? I don't know what I did.

"*Parlami in italiano!*" (Speak to me in Italian!), he insists. I realize that he's never heard me talk to him in English. Apparently, I can never return to English.

Despite our being tired, Katy insists we drive down to Christmas mass at the Basilica. Eilif digs in his heels: "Wait? I can't go into church. I'm a Buddhist!"

We're confused by this sudden proclamation but imagine it's mostly to get out of sitting through a service. Katy reminds Eilif about all the great gifts at home and says that we're just going to wander through the Basilica. He grudgingly agrees that a short visit shouldn't harm his Buddhist principles.

OTTO GETS CAST in the Guthrie Theater's *Christmas Carol.* Eilif thinks he'll be perfect for the role of Tiny Tim since "he looks skinny and malnourished," even if he can eat two giant hamburgers or six tacos at a sitting. Italian friends are pleased he's "Piccolo Tim."

Katy and I are a bit disturbed watching our healthy boy hobble around with a crutch and leg brace. Surprisingly, Otto likes the crippling costume even if he can barely move. What's more, he seems to prefer the Cratchit family to our family as they dote over him and carry him around. They're all so polite with their fake British accents.

I ask Otto if this is the most important event in his life, but I hint that perhaps it was the months we lived in Florence. "Nope, definitely performing at the Guthrie," he responds.

Before his first performance, I tell him that we aren't supposed to say, "Good luck" because it can curse you. Instead, we say, "Break a leg."

He huffs, "That's such a stupid thing to say because my leg is already broken!"

Eilif assures him, "Otto, I'd never tell you to break a leg. Then you'd have two broken legs and that's mean."

Another boy in the play tells Otto, "You know if Tiny Tim were real, I honestly wouldn't care about him." Otto agrees.

Eilif is appalled. "What?! That's the whole point of the play!"

Astri overhears this and asks if the people in the play are real.

I tell her, "They are real, but they're playing characters in the play. Just like Otto is playing Tiny Tim."

Astri thinks a moment, then asks: "Is Otto real?"

Astri doesn't like watching TV, but the next night sees Eilif's show *The Flash.* She asks him, "Are they real?"

"No, they're actors," Eilif confirms.

"Are we actors?" she asks.

"I suppose sometimes," Eilif admits.

"How do you know we're real?" Astri wonders.

Otto theorizes that everything is in our mind anyway, so reality is a construct.

Astri doesn't understand what he's talking about. I try to explain in Italian, but that doesn't help. She then carries on a conversation with herself by making a high, squeaky voice for Sugar Cookie, her stuffed cat, who "asks" her, "Are people real?"

Astri replies to her toy, "Yes . . . and no."

Then she ventriloquizes for Sugar Cookie, who asks about Harry the stuffed dog: "Is Harry real?"

Astri's not sure how to answer her own question and simply looks at her stuffed animals undergoing an existential crisis. Perhaps she thinks they'll disappear if they're not real or we don't believe in them.

I tell her it's time for books before bed, and I read her a Winnie the Pooh story in Italian. I point out that Christopher Robin was a real boy, the son of the author.

"Then who is Winnie the Pooh really?" she asks. "Who is playing Winnie the Pooh?"

I explain: "Winnie the Pooh was Christopher Robin's stuffed animal in these stories. A little like you have Sugar Cookie and Harry."

"Hmm . . . Are we real or are we just in a story?"

# LITTLE ELTON

I trade Italian lessons for Eilif's piano lessons with his music teacher. She plays piano for a children's opera company, so both boys use their Italian as part of the kids' choir for the Minnesota Opera. I worry when Eilif's favorite character in *Tosca* is the sadistic Scarpia. In *La Bohème*, Eilif is a street urchin and has to wear a tag at the practices: "Eilif Dregni: lower class." Otto, on the other hand, is a well-dressed, upper-class snob.

Not all our relatives are convinced opera is so great. Katy offers her dad, Bumpa, free tickets to see the boys in *Tosca*. He replies, "Don't tell them this, but I've succeeded in living my whole life without having to hear Italians sing opera. I really don't know why I should start now."

"OK, I'll give you one 'get-out-of-opera-free' card," Katy concedes. Despite not wanting to see opera, Bumpa comes to any and every other show.

Along with Italian, we want to give the kids skills they can use. We grew nervous when Otto was younger. His teacher asked the children to think of the future and "pledge to dream big!" Otto wrote that he wanted to be a "gamer."

"Great. Just what we need," Katy said.

The following year, he dreams bigger and writes, "I want to be good at air hockey. I want to cross the ocean in a boat." I suppose that's slightly better . . .

When Eilif grows up, he says he wants to be a waiter.

Katy replies, "What? I guess I had some higher aspirations for you."

"Well, I want to be one other thing as well: a musician."

"Um," says Katy. "I kind of hoped you'd do something to make at least some money that would pay your bills while you're a musician."

"What do you want me to be?" Eilif replies full of scorn as he looks at me. "A stupid teacher?"

Otto wants to be a musician too, and I'm pleased they'll finally be able to use their Italian.

Eilif remembers his Italian pronunciation when his first piano teacher tells him that the "ff" on the music score means "fortezemo." Eilif corrects him, "Do you mean '*fortissimo*'?"

Eilif refuses to practice piano. After numerous battles, we tell him we're going to take a break from piano lessons. We even consider getting rid of the piano to free up space in Eilif's tiny room. Eilif dramatically flings his body between us and the piano to save his now beloved instrument. He gives us an ultimatum: "No piano, no Eilif!"

Only then does he play and play and play. He plays so much that Katy is driven crazy by the volume he's able to achieve on our little spinet. The whole house shakes when Eilif bangs the keys. The wooden floors serve as a sounding board for the piano to magnify the sound as if every piece of wood in our house serves as an amplifier.

Katy slips a rug under the legs to soften the sound. She jams rags into the back of the piano to muffle the strings. She considers putting the piano in the garage, even if it would be ruined by the cold. We want to move the piano into the basement, but we'd probably drop it down the steep steps. Katy wears earplugs but then can't communicate with the rest of us. Eilif plays so vigorously that he breaks two piano strings.

Katy decides Otto needs a drum set—perhaps out of equity or to compete against the piano. Incredibly, the drums aren't as loud as the piano, partially because we nestle them down in the basement. Eilif realizes he can play along with the drums on an electric guitar. Of course, he needs to turn up the amplifier and distortion pedal to be heard over the drums.

Katy and I are pleased with the boys' passion for music, but Eilif is not careful with the instruments. "How come each time I play the guitar I break a string?" he asks. Then his verbs become passive, "The guitar was broken"—as if it broke itself.

The next day while I'm glueing instruments at home, we get a call from his music teacher at school: "Eilif broke the piano today. He was showing off by playing with his feet like Elton John."

When Eilif gets home, he's clearly proud of his new reputation at school. He wears oversized sunglasses and outrageous clothes; his classmates nickname him "Elton."

We pay for the piano repair. Eilif brings our keyboard from home to school as a temporary replacement. As he's hauling the big keyboard case, he doesn't have room for his soup for lunch. He stuffs his meal into the case with the keyboard. When he arrives at school, the soup has spilled. He cleans it up the best he can, but tells us, "Now whenever I play, my keyboard smells like soup!"

Because of all his music and acting, Otto gets a role in a play at the History Theater in St. Paul as the son of '60s musician Bobby Vee. The director asks for Otto's bio to print in the playbill, so Katy writes that he plays in a band with his brother.

At opening night, Eilif reads the brochure and is upset to read that he plays in a "rock-n-roll band." "What? We do not play 'rock-n-roll,'" he laments scornfully to Katy.

"Well, what do you play then?" she asks.

"We play alternative, psychedelic art rock!"

They book shows around town and make some money. Otto tells us he might be paid to play drums at a Baptist church for a gospel group.

"Ha ha!" Astri teases him. "You have to go to church!"

Eilif then repeats a joke he heard, "How does a musician make $1,000? Start by giving them $3,000!"

As more musicians file into our basement to jam with the boys, the volume goes up as well. This is rock-n-roll heaven and the loud music shakes the house. "Why do they do this?" Katy asks. "I suppose it's so we won't miss them when they're gone."

## CAESAR MUST DIE

Eilif and Otto are now old enough to be counselors-in-training at Italian camp. Counselors teach not only the language but also the "culture," however we choose to define it. That's where it gets interesting as some American counselors' views of Italy are pop-culture stereotypes.

Ubaldo from Rome demands that we properly represent Italy. He stages a protest and marches around camp with a placard declaring pineapple is not a pizza topping. Ever. He claims Domino's Pizza failed in Italy because of this culinary travesty.

During a weekend break, the American staff make it their mission to have Ubaldo taste pizza topped with pineapple and Canadian bacon. Ubaldo takes a grudging bite. "Hmm, it's delicious," he admits guiltily, "but that doesn't make it right!"

To further immerse the kids in Italian culture, the campers exchange dollars for euros and assume a new Italian name. Astri isn't convinced by her new identity. She asks, "How do I know it's really me?"

Fifteen-year-old Doriana doesn't understand what Italian

camp is about—even after a week: "Where is Italy anyway? Is it that country shaped like a foot or is it the hexagon?"

Her cabinmate answers, "The hexagon is France! I think the long foot is Italy."

Doriana confesses about her hometown: "I don't even know where Minneapolis is on the map . . . I don't even know where we are now . . ."

EILIF ANNOUNCES the theme for the first evening program: a live-action Mario Kart video game based on mustached stereotypes of roly-poly southern Italians. Eilif says sarcastically, "Because Mario Kart is *so* Italian, right?" He knows full well that this is the first view many American kids have of Italians. He plays the character Mario and the counselor Giancarlo is Luigi while the campers run around screaming in delight with cardboard cars and cardboard hammers. The campers suddenly don't miss their cell phones or screen time.

All the yelling and laughing has disturbed the neighboring Arabic camp, however, which has an evening program with kids calmly visiting various displays to learn about adjectives.

The Arabic dean insists, "We have fun too!"

Coco, our nurse, assures her, "I'm sure you do," while she tends to the scraped knees from happy, sweaty participants from this "Italian" video game.

I push the staff for more historically accurate activities, but the kitchen surprises us with Backward Day: spaghetti for breakfast and cereal for dinner. In the past, there was a day based on *la peste nera* (the black plague), but it has become less funny following Covid. Instead we focus on *Inferno* since Hell is always good for laughs. We expose all the different ways we will suffer if we aren't perfectly compliant with biblical warnings. The kids start to understand why our candy store, "*Peccati di Gola*," has a sign flanked with flames and suffering.

"Wait, that means 'sins of the throat'?" Otto notes. "That's weird."

An offended native Italian counselor responds, "*Strano? È Dante!*" (Strange? It's Dante!). The counselor clarifies that one of the seven deadly sins is gluttony, or being *goloso* in Italian, which loosely translates as "throaty." The kids are more confused than ever.

They perk up when Virgil leads Dante through the circles of Inferno. I ask the kids to sit down in the little amphitheater around where we had a campfire the night before. "Oh, a firepit!" Mario says. "Are we going to burn someone alive?"

Little Teodoro exclaims, "God, I hope so!"

We try a program based on the Battle of Troy including a *Cavallo di Troia*, the Trojan horse. Most of the kids know this story. The program isn't too confusing, at least until the Trojan horse's head falls off.

Many of our evening programs devolve into a version of capture the flag. Whether it's the Guelphs versus the Ghibellines or the Fascists versus the Partisans, everyone takes the game very seriously. One camper wears a giant "swamp creature" costume to camouflage as a shrub. His plans are foiled, though, when he can barely walk.

Our business manager says, "To capture the flag, no one thought that Tiziana was nuts enough to venture waist-deep through the muck of the lake to sneak to the other side, but she was!"

When the sun sets, Nina the counselor points out that it's

too dark and the mosquitoes are eating us alive. The campers don't want to stop, though. Ubaldo asks, "Does your team forfeit then?"

A few nights later, Nina introduces an Italian version of capture the flag in which we all have a number attached to a bandanna on our forehead. If the opposing team can see our number and says it (in Italian) out loud, we're captured and must return to base for a new number. We can't cover our number with our hands, so we sneak behind enemy lines hiding our heads behind trees, shrubs, or anything. Our group gets closer to the flag. I'm squatted down with my head tilted sideways behind a garbage can blocking my number. Fourteen-year-old Davide on the enemy team is on the other side of the can. Neither of us dare move to avoid revealing our number. As I'm kneeling with my head against a smelly trash can, Davide calmly asks me, "At this point in your life, is this what you thought you'd be doing?"

A few nights later our theme is warring families: the Montecchi and Capuleti, Dante creations perfected in a play familiar to the kids: *Romeo e Giulietta.* Eilif is playing Romeo, but everyone is worried he'll forget to show up. The afternoon before the performance, Juliet doesn't quite break a leg but sprains her ankle. Coco the nurse gives her crutches so she can hobble around. Capuleto (Lord Capulet) twists his leg playing soccer, so he's limping too. The counselors assign me the role of Montecchi (Lord Montague), but a bee stings me before the play. The play seems doomed when it starts to sprinkle as we perform the secret wedding. One of the Italians proclaims, "*Sposa bagnata, sposa fortunata!*" (A wet bride is a fortunate bride!) It will not end well for Juliet, however.

Another counselor points out that in Shakespeare's play

Romeo is sixteen years old and Juliet is only thirteen, which would be like Eilif/Romeo dating one of the young campers. "Are we promoting child brides?" Fortunately, we sidestep the pedophilia question with a face-off of the Montecchi and Capuleti in a capture the flag match. The lesson we hope they take away is that bullying is bad. Unless you win, of course.

ALONG THE THEME OF BULLIES, we stage the assassination of Julius Caesar, and the staff insist I play Caesar. I wonder if they are actually fantasizing about killing me. To test them, I ask one of the counselors, "Hey Lucia, do you want to be a Roman senator and kill me this evening?"

She's shocked but then realizes that it's part of the evening program. She answers a bit too candidly: "Umm, yes. Yes, I do want to kill you."

I tell the staff that if we stage this, we have to make it look realistic with lots of blood. I dig in the pantry for ketchup, but the counselors say it smells horrible. Instead, they'd already thought ahead and ordered an entire gallon of fake stage blood.

At the staff meeting, I ask if maybe this was really the best use of funds; perhaps a pint would have been plenty.

Lucrezia wisely defends the decision. "Oh no, we'll use it sooner or later."

The label on the bottle of blood declares that it's "edible." I ask, "What are we going to do? Eat it?" I instantly regret saying this as I imagine the counselors planning a program with cannibalistic zombies.

To prepare for my assassination as Caesar, I sit on the dock and fill little plastic bags with stage blood diluted with lake water. I'm surrounded by baggies of blood when I see all the children walk by on the beach on their way to dinner. They wave happily.

In the dining hall, the counselors want to have everyone eat lounging around just like the ancient Romans. We don't have chaise longues or even one sofa. Instead, we fold up all the table legs and lay them flat on the floor. The campers enter the dining hall and are surprisingly good sports about lying down on the sandy floor to eat our food "just like the Romans did!" The kitchen even serves "Roman wine," which is just grape juice with cinnamon. Fourteen-year-old Carmelo, whose father owns a liquor store, takes a sip of the juice and shouts, "This tastes like sweet fireballs! My parents drink it all the time!"

His cabinmate wonders, "Wait, how do you know what fireballs taste like?"

On the beach after dinner the bloodletting begins; the beach is stained red. Eilif is Brutus and stabs me, his father, as Astri watches. They all cheer. Cleopatra screams. The senators flee the site of the crime as I lay in a heap of gore. Mark Antony makes a speech about catching these killers. The campers round up the homicidal senators to bring them to justice, which at camp means throwing them in the lake.

One of the counselors/senators asks them, "Caesar got rid of the Republic to declare himself dictator for life. Weren't we right to kill him?" That nuance of what is justice in this situation is lost on the campers. Instead, they lead all the senators down the dock, as a gangplank, and into the water to their "death."

The assassination of Julius Caesar is such a success that the staff plan an evening program on Caligula. Of course, they insist I play this deranged leader so they can all hate him. As

Caligula, I declare my horse to be a senator but then go even madder. The campers prepare offerings for Caligula, which I promptly burn. I tell them I am, in fact, a god but can't decide whether I'm Mercury, Venus, or Apollo. I just know I hate Neptune and declare war on the lake. I jump in the lake and stab viciously at the water. The campers are confused, but the staff are pleased at the nonsense.

The counselors decide to reenact the founding of Rome. I figured this would be an extension of the Trojan War with Aeneas sailing to Italy to establish Rome. Instead, the counselors jumped right to the story of Romulus and Remus after they suckled from the she-wolf.

Not only did they want to get right to Romulus's murder of his brother Remus, but the counselor Vale proposed doing the *Stupro delle Sabine.*

I double-check to make sure that I understood correctly. I ask, "Are we really doing the Rape of the Sabine Women for an evening program?" I think back to when we saw the statue in Florence and I avoided describing the story to our kids.

Vale defends the decision. "Some say that they actually wanted to go, and it was only the unmarried women, and no one was hurt."

Marco from Milano corrects her: "Um, I don't think there's any controversy that they killed the men and took all their women."

I ask, "So . . . our evening program is about fratricide and abducting women?"

They soften the harsh aspects of the myth and turn the Rape of the Sabine Women into a big game on the soccer field. The kids are divided in two teams, one for Romulus and one for Remus. They gather Skittles and bring them as an offering to me, as the god Jupiter. Meanwhile the Sabine women protect the Skittles with squirt guns since they don't want them to be abducted. As Jupiter, I then decide if Romulus's or Remus's team has gathered the most Skittles to establish Rome.

Little Emilia is relieved and says, "It's nice that no one died today. I was thinking it would happen every day."

As the sun sets, the mosquitoes arrive and dare to accost even me, the king of the gods. For the first time, I'm thankful to be bitten since it puts an end to this strange "historical" program. At least little Enzo is thrilled and declares, "History is fun!"

## CORRUPTING ASTRI

As the director of the Italian camp, I lay down the rules gently not to appear too authoritarian. Many of the Italian staff view my commands as mere "suggestions" anyway, especially Eilif and Otto, who don't listen to me at home and definitely don't now that I'm their boss. The staff will only respect me if I become a mini-Machiavelli.

I note that certain rules are enforced by the American Camp Association, and we must follow them. If the Italian counselors don't like a rule, though, they view it as a challenge. If no one is hurt, who cares?

Agata from Bergamo insists I bring our Australian shepherd to camp. When I tell her it's against the rules and I'd be fired, she scoffs: "You lived in Italy, you know how it works. There are certain rules that you should follow and others that, well, just don't apply to you."

I can't tell if she's joking. She is one of the most honest, hardworking counselors at camp. Astri hears that Agata wants us to bring our dog to camp and is delighted.

"See? Your dog *must* come to camp," Agata winks. "Besides, who would tell? This is *Italian* camp, right? We have many rules in Italy; you choose which ones to obey."

This reminds me of the saying "If you can't be good, be careful!" which Italian priests and monks would say in the Middle Ages, attributing it to St. Paul.

This is a constant theme at Italian camp: the art of "*arrangiarsi*," or figuring out how to work the system. Better yet, making the system work for you. One of our best teachers, Monica from Florence, likes to "borrow" supplies indefinitely from the other language camps. I tell her that we can't do that and at the very least should return the items. She explains that we're doing the camps a favor by putting the supplies to better use since the other camps aren't even using them. In a way, she's right, of course, but would she do the same with someone's speedboat? I explain that I don't want our Italian camp to be viewed as a den of thieves.

"Well, if they don't notice it missing and no one accuses you, it's not really a theft, right?" Monica reasons.

I look around and wonder if I'm missing anything valuable that I didn't notice.

She explains that you need to have supplies in case of emergencies; you might have to escape and leave the country. She whispers to me: "You never know when the time will come!"

I look at her suspiciously and say, "Clearly you've thought a lot about this, I see."

Ubaldo overhears and says (I hope sarcastically), "If you can get away with it, there's no crime, right? Just like if they can't find the body, it's not really a murder."

I told them that I overheard the camper Georgia saying that she could do anything she wants: "It's a free country!"

Her cabinmate Francesca corrected her, "Well, it's not free-free. I mean, you can't rob a bank." Fortunately, Ubaldo and

Monica hadn't overheard this conversation. They would probably make the kids side with the thieves stealing from the rich bankers to help the poor. I could imagine them asking, "Isn't it OK to rob a bank as long as you get away with it?"

DESPITE THIS PENCHANT to look the other way, the native Italian teachers are painfully honest when they evaluate the high school kids who come for a month to take language classes. A teacher from northern Italy writes that her student Carolina "does not show dedication to improving" and should maybe give up even trying. Before we can stop the teacher, she sends this note home. Her parents are shocked. I try to explain to them that in Italian schools, participation points don't count; the students have to prove themselves to the teacher.

Whenever the teachers give written feedback to the parents, the Minnesotan staff must soften the Italians' writing—perhaps to be more passive-aggressive. Still, the native Italian staff insist on "telling the truth." In evaluations, they are used to the Italian system that makes students have to show they are worthy rather than teachers encouraging kids with positive reinforcement.

One teacher complains after she reads over our softened version: "What is that? You're just inflating their egos when they need to know the truth!"

More than once, the teachers' harsh reviews of students are sent home, and I have to talk the parents down. I don't bother explaining that when I was a high school student in Brescia, my Italian classmates viewed it as their duty to band together to help each other pass exams. Sure, this may be cheating by our puritanical American standards, but the solidarity against the tyranny of the teachers' system brings a sense of community for all the students. I wonder if parents will just view our camp as either corrupting their kids or teaching them to survive in a corrupt world.

ONE EVENING after a two-hour meal, we ask the kids to return to their cabins to get dressed up before coming back to the dining hall. Little Francesca complains, "Don't tell me we're going to eat again?"

"No, we're going to gamble!" Isabella responds.

Eilif and Giancarlo have organized casino night.

The campers put on their fanciest outfits as the casinos in Italy are black-tie affairs for the elite. I point out the historical connection that the world's first casino opened in Venice in 1638. Astri doesn't care and views this as a chance to get rich quick. Even if it's just Monopoly money.

Little Francesca tells Astri, "My dad says that gambling is a tax on the stupid."

Nina the counselor assures Little Francesca that her dad is a wise man, but tonight we risk it all. The staff feel like they're getting the kids ready for the real world, or at least for Italy. "We invented cheating," the teacher Carlotta from Ravenna informs me. Archaeologists even found ancient, weighted dice in the Colosseum; spectators would gamble in the stands in between the slaughters. The Italian staff assure me that gambling is "culturally appropriate."

The campers enter the "*casinò*" to find tables of blackjack, roulette, *tombola,* and scopa. Eilif plays the piano to provide a high-class, lounge atmosphere to the impending chaos while other counselors serve cocktails of grape juice to the young patrons. Each cabin group is given a wad of photocopied Monopoly bills, "euros," and one hour to get rich at the games.

I play ping-pong—whoever can win the best out of five points against me doubles their money. The counselor Giancarlo gathers their bets, and most kids lose. Only the camper Mario can beat me.

Giancarlo then lets the kids bet on me to double their money. The campers realize that if they put up a bad player, they can bet on me and win big. Astri and several campers intentionally lose their games against me and get rich.

I want a rematch with Mario, who beat me last time. Giancarlo announces that anyone can triple their money on this five-point match. Mario has a huddle with his cabinmates. They place all their money on me to win. Giancarlo gathers a giant wad of Monopoly money as most of the campers have staked their gambling fortunes on me. I'm flattered that they think I'm such a good ping-pong player, especially considering Mario won the last match.

Mario serves the ball and makes an atypical mistake. The first point goes to me.

Giancarlo leans over and whispers, "Don't you see what they're doing? You have to lose!"

Mario's next serve makes it over the net, but I "accidentally" smash the ball off the ceiling. Everyone is stunned as I lose two points in a row. It's a race to the bottom as Mario tries to play worse than I do.

"The game is fixed!" little Isabella shouts. "I know since I'm from Queens and we know all about this."

The score is 2–2 and whoever loses the next point is the "winner." It's my serve and I intentionally miss the serve by about ten feet. The room erupts with shouts of "*Ingiustizia!*"

"*Ladri!*" "*Imbroglioni!*" (Injustice! Thieves! Cheaters!) I'm mostly impressed that they've learned this vocabulary.

"The house always wins," Giancarlo explains. One of the counselors "secretly" gives a wad of fake euros to Mario to breed suspicion that he was in on it all along.

Little Francesca sums it up: "This is all about who can cheat the best."

Just as the campers calm down, Giancarlo stops the game and asks if everyone is indeed old enough to gamble: "No? You must be eighteen to gamble in Italy. If you're not, you have to pay *tangenti*," or bribes.

Little Gianna doesn't quite understand, but exclaims, "I don't understand the context, but I *love* blackmail!"

The counselor Nina coos, "*Adesso mi sento a casa.*" (Now I feel at home.)

Agata seems proud that the kids have become *furbo* (sly). They're now smart enough to realize that every game is rigged. They have to be one step ahead to survive. They've finally learned the art of *arrangiarsi*, or working the system.

"Gambling is fun!" little Antonio proclaims. "I'm gonna be a gambling addict when I grow up."

"*Voglio corrompere tua figlia!*" (I want to corrupt your daughter!), Nina from Torino tells me with a menacing grin.

"What?" I ask. "Why would you want to do that? Astri's only eleven years old." I'm worried that their lessons in "true" Italian culture have gone too far.

Nina approaches Astri to inquire if she knows the location of my new cabin. I just changed cabins to a remote one all alone and want to keep it secret so everyone won't come looking for me in the middle of the night for supposed emergencies. Not even Astri knows where it is, but now she desperately wants in on the "secret."

I whisper the location in Astri's ear. I make her put her hand over her heart and promise—*ti giuro!*—that she won't tell anyone.

Now that Astri knows, Nina pretends she really wants to know. Nina could care less where my cabin is; she just wants Astri to spill her secret. To corrupt Astri.

Nina begins with reverse psychology. "I don't care where your papà sleeps now," she states.

"*Va bene*," OK, Astri replies, and walks away.

Nina attempts a different tactic. She lies triumphantly, "I know where your papà's new cabin is!"

"Oh, that's good," Astri responds, uninterested.

Nina can't stand it, so she flat out admits that she desperately wants to know the secret. Astri is nervous but excited that this information is valuable.

"She wanted a bribe!" Nina reports to me. "She demanded another piece of focaccia."

"Well, what did you do? Teach her that asking for bribes is wrong?"

"Oh no, I gave her the focaccia, and she told me everything. I corrupted her!"

I'm worried that I've done just as much to "corrupt" the kids. At dinner, we have the *guida misteriosa*, a random "mystery counselor" who watches and listens to see which camper speaks the most Italian during the day. The day that I'm the mystery counselor, as a joke, I award the prize to myself—and righteous cries of outrage force me to give up the prize.

The next day, our nurse Coco is too busy to dress up as the

patron saint of cleanliness, Santa Zita, and give the prize to the cleanest cabin as she normally does. I dress up in her costume and jokingly award myself again, even though no one knows where my cabin is.

I ask Nina if I'm a terrible example by joking how supposedly unethical we "Italians" are. "Oh no, I feel much more at home with this," Nina assures me.

I realize it's a team effort to wise up Astri and the others to not believe everything—or anything really. Nina explains that before the focaccia bribe, she was trying to earn Astri's confidence. Astri tells her, "I'm a better ice skater than Papà, even if he always says he's better." Nina confirms that she doesn't truly believe anything I say. "Me neither!" Astri agrees enthusiastically. "I never believe him."

When I see Astri, I ask her if she revealed our secret about my new cabin's whereabouts. "No!" she exclaims, a bit offended that I would even ask. She notices that Nina is right there and backtracks: "Oh . . . yes . . . well . . . but Nina *really* wanted to know!"

Lucrezia overhears our exchange and informs me that Nina is doing us a favor: "Astri will always question what people say rather than have to be hurt and resentful when she finds out they're liars."

ONE SUNDAY MORNING, several of the staff complain that our prime minister at Italian camp isn't doing her job: "She's late!" "She plays favorites!"

I'm not sure what is going on or whom they consider the "prime minister." Is that . . . me? I can tell the counselors have planned an insurrection or perhaps a coup. Nina tells me that

I'm the president and Lucrezia, the assistant dean, is the *primo ministro*, who is neither lazy nor late.

Regardless, the counselors call for a vote of confidence after breakfast. After damning speeches about the inefficiency of our political system at camp, the campers give a vote of *sfiducia*, or no confidence, to oust Lucrezia. Only Otto dares go against the grain and votes to keep her as he can see this is all nonsense.

Far from offended, Lucrezia is thrilled that she can finally take a day off and do her laundry. She hands me her resignation since I'm apparently the *presidente della repubblica* as the counselors make me don a suit and tie. Meanwhile, former Prime Minister Lucrezia sleeps in the hammock on the beach. I wonder if I could resign to take a nap too.

With the power vacuum at Italian camp, six political parties strive to gain control. It's Machiavelli Day. All parties vie for power with a logo, motto, and platform. One demands that we add six hours of free time and naps to each day.

I'm confused: "Wait, you want a thirty-hour day?"

"Yes!" they cheer emphatically.

Mostly the parties demand more Nutella. Another party, *La Federazione della Nutella*, insists we serve Nutella at every meal. Otto gives an impassioned speech about the benefits of Nutella to raucous cheers. The kitchen staff is appalled because they're sick of scraping off plates covered with this gooey, gluey hazelnut spread. Negotiations break down and the kitchen goes on *sciopero*, or strike, against Nutella—complete with placards depicting crossed-out Nutella jars.

The ex–prime minister, Lucrezia, fresh back from her nap, points out to the kitchen staff that the time for a strike is when the government is *still* in power. Otto's Nutella Federa-

tion doesn't hear her since they're too busy chanting. In fact, everyone is chanting, and no one is listening.

The number of parliamentary seats each party holds depends not only on the number of votes but on how well their followers do in a potato sack race, a marathon, and a paper airplane toss through Hula-Hoops. The counselors argue that this isn't a bad way to determine the survival of the fittest. The final competition involves passing a plate of flour backward over their heads and results in campers covered in a fine flour dusting as though ready to be fried. When they jump in the lake to clean off, we remember that flour and water make glue.

The counselors count the ballots and tally the results of the competitions, but no party has a mandate. Just as in Italy, bizarre coalitions form: The party promoting an extended day of napping makes peace with the Nutella Federation. Each insists their own candidate become prime minister.

After a long debate and many votes, the largest coalition announces that their new prime minister will be the youngest in the group: "Astri!"

"Corruption!" shouts Nina. "The daughter of the *presidente della repubblica* is the prime minister? How does that happen?"

I argue that Nina was the one who corrupted her, but she assumes that I paid off the coalition somehow.

"How is this not nepotism?" she asks and demands new elections.

Fortunately, it's time for *lasagne* and everyone is starving. No one listens to Nina's call for an investigation into fraud since everyone likes little Astri.

The kitchen staff has stopped their strike and somehow Astri gets credit for making peace. She surpasses expectations knowing how to keep everyone happy: Her first act as prime minister is to order the kitchen to give everyone ice cream—and she gets all the credit. Machiavelli would be proud.

## WHERE TO NOW?

As Eilif goes to college, Katy declares, "I'm done parenting. I'm really done."

"Umm, Astri is only thirteen and Otto is just finishing high school," I remind her. We are both tired and dream that the kids can just manage on their own. Once you start parenting, you can't get out of it. Some years ago, they didn't exist, but now we can't imagine life without them. As much as we complain, we'd tackle a grizzly bear to save them.

At night, Katy wakes up worrying. I hear an audible, "Oh my God!" but I've learned to keep sleeping. In the morning, she lists some of the reasons she keeps waking up: (1) Otto bought gum, but the orthodontist put a retainer in his mouth. (2) How do you figure out the square footage of a room? (3) What *is* blood pressure?

We hear that teachers in the Minneapolis Public Schools are going on strike. "Why should they be able to," Katy wonders, "since parents can never go on strike?"

We can only watch as the kids follow their dreams. Otto's bassoon will take him to southern Italy with his orchestra and France soon afterward. Who knows where Astri's hockey will take her?

I like to think that Eilif's time in Florence was the impetus for him to go to the Minneapolis College of Art and Design. When the school suggests he sign up to study for a semester in Florence at the Accademia di Belle Arti (where Michelangelo's *David* lives), Eilif sighs, "I've already done that." Instead, he takes four semesters of Japanese to prepare to go to Japan. He's disillusioned with the teaching, though. "We just have a lesson for an hour and then we're expected to know the material!"

"You're supposed to study," I respond.

"They don't do any repetition, so these classes don't work for me."

I realize he's been spoiled by immersion at the language camps and my years of blabbing at him in Italian. He signs up to be a counselor at Japanese camp and jumps right into conversing with the other counselors and leading sing-alongs. He plans to go Japan.

WE WATCH OUR KIDS STRUGGLE and sometimes succeed. I tell them that life isn't a straight path but more of a crooked line with potholes along the way. We want to clear the path for them—become "snowplow parents"—but they must find their own way. They insist on it even when we give advice. We just hope that we've given them the tools and an opening to the world.

I wish our time in Italy had instilled them with the travel bug, but they seem perfectly content being back among friends and relatives in Minnesota. They are worldly and don't need to be in another country to realize what is important. Perhaps they learned the Italian lesson that *la famiglia è tutto*, family is everything, because *chi si volta, chi si gira, sempre a casa va finire*, or "home is where the heart is."

---

I ASK KATY if she'll read over this manuscript about our time parenting. "Why would I want to read that when I lived it?" she asks. "Besides, it'll just make me mad since you always make yourself out to be so doe-eyed and innocent rather than how you really are."

I ask her, jokingly, "How am I really?"

"Do you need to ask?"

"Umm, maybe . . ." I say.

"Well, do you really want me to tell you?"

"Maybe not . . ."

"What do you think it's like to live with a spy?" Katy asks. "You use everything I say against me." I explain that she's funny and quotable. She says she wants to write about how we lose ourselves when we have kids and call it "What the Hell Happened?" She never has time to write it, though.

"I don't remember anything, just that there was lots of joy and heartbreak," she admits. "It's been a fog. I don't have one damn memory!"

Katy turns to the kids. "You have got to get it together because one of these days I'm going to check out. Then it's all up to you."

Astri asks, "Papà, what happens if you and Mamma die? Then Eilif and Otto die? Where will I go?" Katy assures her that many people would love to have her. She gives Astri a bear hug.

She asks Katy, "Would I go to Jean's?"

"Maybe . . ."

"Hurray! Then I can have another cat!"

# EPILOGUE

## Sicilian Dreams

Buy a house in Sicily for one euro?

We've seen the news stories about dying towns in southern Italy selling houses for almost nothing if the new owners fix them up. Katy and I dream of packing up our three kids and moving to that fabled island with crystal blue seas.

Its reputation as birthplace of the Mafia must be overblown, right? Friends in northern Italy warn us about the south. "*Attenzione!*" They'd gently pull down their lower eyelid, a warning gesture that everyone is *furbo*, a sneaky wiseguy. Only Giovanni from Milano knows this is nonsense and that Palermo is fantastic. He concedes that we Americans always fear a fedora-wearing mafioso is lurking in every Sicilian alley.

Our friend Serafino from Messina scoffs at the worried northerners, assuring us Sicily is the best part of Italy. I reveal to him my dream of renting Italian scooters and spending a month zooming around the island.

"Are you crazy? The Vespas would be stolen the first day!"

We book our flights when we learn that Otto's youth orchestra is going on a dream tour to southern Italy. We'll be groupies at the Sicilian shows. We also realize this might be our last family trip since the boys will leave home soon.

Instead of Vespas, we opt for planes, trains, and daredevil bus drivers weaving up the winding roads. The too-small guardrails would do nothing to stop us from plunging into the Ionian Sea.

Rather than reserving a hotel, should we just buy a one-euro house? Then we remember the mountains of indecipherable paperwork from when Katy and I merely rented an apartment in Modena for a couple of years.

To overcome the Kafkaesque Italian labyrinth of documents when we lived in Modena, we made friends with people in the *questura*, or police station. We nervously walked by the guards with their machine guns and prayed they had the safety on as they puffed their cigarettes. Inside the *questura*, I told them I was writing for the newspaper and teaching. "If there's any trouble, we know where you are!" they joked—supposedly—and then wondered if they could get lessons in English. They let us stay in Modena for three years as long as we "helped out."

If we bought a house in Sicily, how many lawyers, notaries, carpenters would we have to pay to purchase a house? Italian friends in the Twin Cities cite the impossible bureaucracy as a top reason they left Italy.

Will we need citizenship? Some friends bought a place in Porto, Portugal, with plans of getting European citizenship, but Italy offers no such deals. I have asked people at the Italian consulate in Chicago if the government could help promote our Italian summer camp. They respond with indifference: "Everyone wants to go to Italy, so why is that necessary?" Perhaps callous, but are they wrong?

Instead of purchasing (and renovating) a boondoggle in a remote, sun-scorched southern town where we could legally stay for only three months a year on a tourist visa, we rent a villa in Taormina and imagine it as our own. (I ignore that our entire trip costs more than buying that one-euro house and beginning restorations.) We want to feel what it is like to live there and cook our food at home—even if the kids would prefer to eat gelato three meals a day.

We climb four flights of steps on the edge of town to "our" villa. This isn't the arid landscape of a spaghetti western set with Clint Eastwood chewing a stubby cigar and prickly pears as the only greenery. No, Taormina is lush with lemon trees, bitter orange, African violets in three shades of purple, and star jasmine with an aroma that makes me swoon.

The caretaker, Roberto, tells us to pick the parsley, basil, rosemary, oregano, and wild fennel from the garden. He apologizes that the figs aren't ripe and the almonds need a few more weeks.

Enthralled by the garden, we haven't even noticed the view of the azure sea merging with the sky. "That's Calabria over there," Roberto says, pointing to where the toe of the big boot stands ready to kick Sicilia out of Italy. Mount Etna is to the south, and the Greek amphitheater from 300 BCE is perched on the edge of the cliff.

The kids run through the garden and Astri screams when she sees a black snake. We ask the gardener if it's poisonous. "Oh yes, vipers are poisonous. If you don't touch it, you probably won't get bitten." We tell the kids not to pet the snakes.

---

Katy mentions to Roberto that she read that the best gelato in Italy is from a small town in central Sicily.

Roberto scoffs, "That must be a mistake. Where did you hear that?"

"CNN," Katy replies.

"That journalist must have been paid off to write that!" Roberto assures us. "You must try the gelato in Taormina first, then tell me what you think."

On the main drag, we noticed "Gelatomania" with more than fifty flavors of gelato—but Sicily is more famous for granita. While Richard Burton and Elizabeth Taylor spent their days at the Wunderbar in Taormina drinking and arguing, the Bam Bar is where Francis Ford Coppola, Richard Dreyfuss, and other VIPs drown their sorrows in granita.

At the Bam Bar, granita is hardly a chunky, granular snow cone with syrup, but a silky, smooth shaved-ice delight infused with everything from peaches to melon, pistachios to almonds. To avoid overheating in the morning in sunny Sicily, the classic hot Italian breakfast of a *cornetto* (croissant) and cappuccino is replaced with a frozen granita and eggy brioche. The kids badger us to go every morning. Of course, Astri orders granita with Nutella.

All life and death in eastern Sicily is thanks to Etna, Roberto tells us. Even granita and gelato can be credited to the nearly eleven-thousand-foot active volcano. "Arabs brought the idea for granita north across the Mediterranean, but the Sicilians perfected it," the owner of Bam Bar tells me. The Greeks as well gathered snow and ice from Etna and stored it in caves to have for summer treats.

---

Etna looms over everything, as if ready to destroy this paradise, just as Vesuvius did with Pompeii and Herculaneum. Roberto tells me that sometimes Etna rains down fire, or if they were lucky just breccia, fine pebbles that fall from the sky and sit like cement on roofs but is a natural fertilizer full of minerals. Etna kills but also gives life, which makes Taormina a verdant Garden of Eden.

Anything blooms here, especially pistachios. We find pistachio honey, pistachio granita, pistachios in cheese, pistachios in baloney, pistachio pesto, and pistachios on cannoli and pizza. Even the local butcher has special *involtini*, beef rolls stuffed with pistachios and soft cheese. When I don't have enough euros, the butcher insists I just pay next time, even if we're leaving the next day. He just wants to make sure I taste his handiwork.

Our last evening in Taormina, Otto's orchestra plays at the Greek amphitheater as the sun sets and the pillars onstage frame Mount Etna. As the musicians pack up after the concert, the trombonists strike up some standards and Eilif jumps on stage to accompany them on piano for an impromptu after-hours jazz session. I ask the piano mover if he needs them to stop, but he won't hear of it: "Why would I stop a party?"

An Italian chaperone asks Astri, "Do you play? Are you a musician like your brothers?"

Astri is a disgusted, "No! I play hockey."

THE TRAIN FROM TAORMINA TO PALERMO weaves along the coast of the pristine Tyrrhenian Sea. After three hours, the train inches to a stop in a field outside the town of Bagheria. *Sciopero!* Strike! The conductor explains some rail workers demanded better pay and walked out during a "hiccup" strike.

I ask him about the bathroom on this super modern train since the display light always shows it as occupied. He tells me, "*Funziona, ma non bene.*" (It works, but not well.) "You have to hold the door shut and it will probably overflow."

After an hour to show the power of the workers, the train squeaks forward into Palermo. We walk around the labyrinth of the city center, looking for dinner. The delicious is mixed in with the odd: skewers of grilled lamb intestines and "horse balls" (meatballs made from horsemeat). Do you like to eat your spleen with or without cheese? A line forms down the block for a steaming cauldron of snails. Hmm, intriguing, but not exactly kid-friendly.

In the north of Italy, I have never seen cannoli and only heard of these Sicilian delights through southern Italian immigrants in the United States. In Palermo, we line up for "holy cannoli" made by the cloistered nuns of St. Catherine. I was about to point out to the kids how peaceful living in a convent

or monastery would be, but I remember how St. Catherine of Alexandria was martyred: being strapped to a giant wheel that tortured her with each turn. When the wheel broke, Emperor Maxentius just lopped off her head. Perhaps St. Catherine was having her vengeance for my heretical thoughts when eating the cannoli in the peaceful garden turns into a ricotta mess.

Our favorite meal is also the cheapest: user-friendly *sfincione*, a sort of Sicilian pizza with caramelized onions that feeds the family for six euros. We eat on the street with revelers in the twelfth-century Vucciria market.

All the northerners' worries about mafiosi in Sicily are clearly overblown—the only danger we see is dodging the classic restored Piaggio Ape cars, essentially three-wheeled Vespas that no one is trying to steal. The people hanging out in Palermo alleys are having their evening *aperitivo*, sitting on doorsteps and chatting with friends after the day's heat has dissipated. The maze of narrow streets is one long *festa* and everyone is invited.

For a month after our trip, I dream I'm still in Taormina. Maybe navigating all the bureaucracy to buy a house here would be worth it after all.

On our way home from Sicily, our flight stops in Rome. Katy insists we bring the kids to the Vatican. I ask her if she really wants to do this after our experiences at the Basilica in Minneapolis when the kids were little. Did she remember Eilif and Otto singing Sunday school songs on the playground about God and Jesus saving us all? At the time, Katy shrank down on the park bench, worried that the other parents would think we're religious zealots.

"We're in Rome. They have to go to the Vatican," she says. "Besides, it's all these people that talk about God that I can't stand. Sure, I believe in God, but I never trust anyone who says they do."

Astri hears us talking and asks her brother, "Otto, do you believe in God?"

"Hmm, I think I'm more agnostic," Otto ponders.

"What? That's not true!" Astri says. "You do too eat eggs!"

"No, it's 'AG-nostic' not 'EGG-nostic.' 'Eggnostic' is not a word."

"Yes, it is!" insists Astri who then asks our phone. "Alexa . . . is 'egg-nostic' a word?"

Alexa responds, "Yes, *agnostic* means someone who . . ."

"See! I'm right again!" Astri declares triumphantly.

Otto shakes his head. "I am not *egg*-nostic."

"Aha! So you do eat eggs after all. Got you again!"

Otto has to stay with his orchestra tour, but the rest of us go through the long line into St. Peter's. Astri reads one of the calendars there and points out "Good Friday," or *venerdì santo.* "Papà! That's Good Friday. Isn't that great?" she tells me.

"Well, you know that it's not so 'good.'"

"Wait, why?"

"This is the day the Romans nailed Jesus to the cross and he stayed there until he died."

Katy explains, "Yes, but I suppose that's why they say it's 'good,' since he took away our sins."

Eilif adds, "I guess that sucks for Jesus but is great for us."

Astri points to a painting with Jesus sitting beside twelve men. "Who were those guys?"

"Those were the apostles," Katy points out, "who helped Jesus."

"He had twelve personal assistants?" Astri says. "I want a personal assistant."

I point out that as parents we are essentially her personal assistants.

Astri shakes her head, "Well, you're not doing a very good job!"

We enter the atrium of the basilica, and I point out the Porta Santa on the right entrance that is bricked up until the next Jubilee. At that time, the pope ceremoniously hammers a hole into it so pilgrims may walk through and cleanse their sins. Eilif thinks the whole idea is silly: "The poor ol' pope has to knock down all those bricks by himself! Poor guy."

Inside St. Peter's, Eilif seems overcome by the grandeur of the church. He leans onto a bench and stares up at the altar and cupola for about ten minutes. I point this out to Katy who whispers, "It's about damn time!"

A priest recites mass in the front of the church, but a guard won't let the tourists join. Katy tells him she's Catholic and that we're here to pray. He allows the four of us to the front. I reluctantly follow with Astri and Eilif and sit in the pews. Impressively, Katy knows all the gestures and prayers.

Eilif donates twenty euros to the church but then needs more money. He tells me, "That's what money is for, right?"

Astri asks me about the Eucharist. I whisper that church-goers believe that it is not just a wafer but literally the body of Christ. "Eww! That's disgusting! They eat Jesus?"

I explain how the wine changes too. "What? They drink blood?"

Six teenage boys in front of us dutifully cross themselves with no adults present. Strange. They take Communion but they bring the wafer, the host, back to their pew. A Vatican guard swiftly comes to insist they finish eating the wafer. Katy whispers to me, "Christ will not leave the building!"

She then approaches the altar to receive the Eucharist and tells us to wait behind. Eilif won't hear of it and gets in line further behind her. She notices, furiously gesturing for him to sit down, all while trying not to make a scene. He won't budge.

They both return to the pews. Katy thinks Eilif is being disrespectful as he licks his lips and says, "I'm in the Vatican doing Communion. How dope is that?"

ON THE WAY BACK on the plane, I ask the kids if they're now planning on returning to Italy, perhaps to study art or fashion or food. "*No . . . probabilmente no,*" Astri replies, oblivious to all the effort we put into taking them abroad.

Well . . . will you at least sign up for Italian classes to become truly fluent?

"*Perché?* We already speak it."

I wonder what the point of all of this was. Were all the classes, summer camp, and trips in vain? Then I remember that my parents brought my brothers and me to live in Belgium when I was little. I attended French school in first grade but soon enough forgot most of the language. I tell Astri that perhaps I should stop speaking Italian to her and switch to my flawed French . . . or my mediocre Norwegian.

"Sure, French will be easy after Italian," she responds with swagger. I'm speechless as I remember all those hours memorizing French verb charts and mispronouncing the guttural vowels to the horror of my teachers. I let Astri believe she can conquer French and do anything she can dream of since soon enough life will humble even the bravest of us.

I imagine my parents had very different plans for my future and probably wanted me to return to study in Belgium after we had lived there for two years. That never happened, but the experience formed me and opened my mind to other cultures. When we moved back to suburbia, I knew there was life beyond our borders and ended up in Italy. Every time I travel there, I want to return for more.

As the kids sleep on the long flight home, I wonder how they'll look back on these trips and growing up in two cultures. I wonder what they'll do when they grow up and what adventures they'll have. Where will they live and who will they love? Perhaps they will pass on an experience like this in a completely different country. I imagine them with their future families navigating the world and constantly surprised by their kids who are afraid of nothing.

# ACKNOWLEDGMENTS

To my family, who were the guinea pigs in becoming bilingual; and to my parents and brothers, who put up with this bizarre experiment. Thank you to Tiziana, the best proofreader ever, who convinced me that this book should go to press. Thanks to the *Star Tribune* (especially Simon Peter Groebner) for publishing portions of my travel essays.

Thanks especially to the University of Minnesota Press, especially Erik Anderson, Heather Skinner, Emma Saks, and Alena Rivas, for making this book happen; Concordia University for sending me to Italy and providing a Quasi Endowment Grant that helped fund my writing of this book; and the Concordia Language Villages (especially Fie) for continuing to believe that learning languages expands our world.

So many others tolerated becoming "characters" in the book by sharing their insights: Anna and Giovanni Erba from Milano, Guido, Serafino, Vicki Barker, Carol Berg, Julie Schumacher, Margaret, Annie and Grace, Jean, Fede in Florence, Sheila from Climax, and Roberto in Taormina. *Grazie mille* to all those who came on my trips to Italy and to Lago del Bosco: Agata, Alex, Alice, Alpina, Anna, Carlo and Rosa, Carolina, Coco, Doriana, Emilia, Enzo, Francesca, Georgia, Giancarlo, Isabella, Kelly, Leo, Letizia, Lucia, Lucrezia, Lupo, Marco, Monica, Natasha, Nina, Paola, Ubaldo, Vale, Vera, and many more . . .

**ERIC DREGNI** is professor of English, journalism, and Italian at Concordia University St. Paul and the dean of the Italian Concordia Language Village, Lago del Bosco. He lives in Minneapolis and often leads trips to Italy. He is the author of twenty-two books, including *In Cod We Trust, Never Trust a Thin Cook, Vikings in the Attic*, and *You're Sending Me Where? Dispatches from Summer Camp*, all published by the University of Minnesota Press.